my favourite
cheap eats

Calgary, Banff, Canmore, Foothills, and beyond

For Joan + Mike

Let's Eat!

[signature]

John Gilchrist

edited by Catherine Caldwell

Escurial Incorporated
Calgary, Alberta

© 2008, John Gilchrist

Published by
Escurial Incorporated
9519 Assiniboine Road SE
Calgary, Alberta
Canada T2J 0Z5
Phone: (403) 255·7560
Email: escurial@telus.net

Library and Archives Canada Cataloguing in Publication

Gilchrist, John, 1953 –
    My favourite cheap eats : Calgary, Banff, Canmore, Foothills, and beyond / John Gilchrist ; edited by Catherine Caldwell.

ISBN: 978–0–9693106–6–2

1. Restaurants—Alberta—Calgary Region—Guidebooks. 2. Calgary Region (Alta.)—Guidebooks. I. Caldwell, Catherine, 1956 – II. Title.
TX907.5.C22A43 2008   647.957123'38   c2008–900684–4

CREDITS:
Interior Design: Jeremy Drought, Last Impression Publishing Service, Calgary, Alberta
Cover Design: Pierre Lamielle, Calgary, Alberta
Printed and bound in Canada by Friesens Corporation, Altona, Manitoba

Contents

Acknowledgements

CATHERINE and I looked at a wealth of designs for the cover of this book before deciding on the simple (and hopefully elegant-but-cheap) black-and-white theme. That Pierre Lamielle is one heck of a creative (and patient) designer. We want to thank him for his great work and mention that he is a heck of a cook too.

We also want to thank friends Brenda and Richard White who have become our go-to brainstormers on cover images. We like their no-nonsense approach, which generates non-stop ideas. (And how about our other friends and family who put up with us hijacking social gatherings with book talk?)

A big bow also to Jeremy Drought, our talented (and also patient) interior book designer. How someone can know so much about fonts and layout and kerning (what is kerning anyway?) is beyond us. This is his fourth book for us, and we both expect to be working with him again in the near future.

Here's a shout-out to Andrew Wedderburn, too, for providing the entertaining Foreword. We feel fortunate that he joined us. He's a talent, and we want to say we knew him when. If you haven't read his first novel, *The Milk Chicken Bomb,* do so. It was the best thing I read in 2007. (And I read as much as I eat.)

For my part, let me not forget the indefatigable Catherine, my charming spouse whose graceful edits dot these pages. Without her, I'm a gibbering nit. (She pulls a mean espresso too.)

And last, thank you dear reader (and eater) for allowing me to play with my food.

Foreword

by Andrew Wedderburn

THERE isn't much that grows out of the ground or pecks around the bottom of the coop that human ingenuity hasn't managed to bacon-wrap, deep-fry, and serve in wax paper. It's up to each of us to find a reasonably clean, under-ten-dollar corner (preferably with a swivelling vinyl stool) to eat it all, one paper-plate-sized portion at a time.

You may need help in your quest. At my favourite breakfast counter,* I'm known affectionately as Three Egg Sunny-Side No Meat. If they know my actual, nothing-to-do-with-breakfast name, it's never come up. You're probably someone's Three Egg Sunny-Side No Meat too if you care at all about squeezing the most possible melted cheese for the fewest possible dollars into every single day. (Although you likely eat sausage and enjoy life more than I do.) Somewhere you've discovered that perfect late night pizza window where your favourite slice is always just coming out of the oven, or the ideal shawarma stand where everybody knows your order. If not, take heart: John Gilchrist knows them all, and he's ready to share.

Sure, they're knocking the whole city down around our ears. You may well have seen your favourite spot bulldozed over the last year, or maybe rebranded as a contemporary urban fusion bistro. But time is on our side. Our little chunk of the world is bulging at the seams with new arrivals from every culinary time zone. They want takeout pakoras, roti shops, burek, and anything that can be slowed down long enough to deep-fry on a stick. Eating cheap is its own reward—a really good box of hot soba noodles can taste like it cost you $40. And with the money you'll save eating them all the time, you can head over to that new contemporary urban fusion bistro and have something with truffle oil that really costs $40. In the meantime, there's always plenty of table space in Chinatown. I'll see you there—we can split the salt-and-pepper squid.

* No, I'm not telling—it's hard enough to get a table in there. Read the book and go hang out at John's favourite diner.

Andrew Wedderburn is a vocalist and guitarist for the Calgary-based indie band Hot Little Rock and the author of The Milk Chicken Bomb. *If you see him at a book signing, ask to borrow his pen.*

Introduction

Some people call me cheap. Not many really, just my family, most of my friends, and various casual acquaintances. Personally, I consider myself to be "value conscious," aware of a good deal when I see one. I attribute this to my oddly hybridized Scottish-Swedish-Central-Alberta-agrarian upbringing.

So when it comes to finding a good lunch for under $15 or dinner for under $20, I'll search high and low. Because they're out there. I've found over 150 independent cafes, restaurants, espresso bars, bakeries, buses, buffets, shacks, and other indefinable food-service outlets that I think do a decent job. So here they are—I hope you enjoy them too.

First, though, a few words of clarification:

- Generally, entries in this book serve lunch for under $15, dinner for under $20, or a good breakfast at a good price. In most, though, you can also exceed the budget, so dine carefully.
- All the entries (well, most of them) are arranged alphabetically. (The ones on pages 110 to 115 are not. They are what I call the "More" entries—places for which I didn't have enough room to dedicate a whole page or places that didn't fit my cheap-eats price definition entirely or places I just like and wanted to include. And there are a few more rogue entries too confusing to explain here. (I can hear the teeth-gnashing from my editor and library-technician wife.) Suffice it to say that The Lists at the back have *see* references that shall make it all clear.)
- All phone numbers start with 403 if you're calling long distance.
- All entries are non-smoking. (Hurray!)
- When I include Delivery in the sidebar under the Takeout category, there are always limitations on this, such as how far away from the eatery you are or how much food you ordered.
- Sidebar abbreviations for credit cards are: **AE** for American Express, **V** for Visa, and **MC** for MasterCard.
- Again in the sidebar, this time under the Drinks category, Corkage means you can bring a bottle of wine you purchased elsewhere (no homemade hooch, though). It also means you can take the remainder of an unfinished bottle of wine with you when you leave.

So, you can call me cheap. I don't mind at all. Remember, it takes one to know one.

*atomic

Urban Tea & Subs

I<small>N</small> this book, you will find many small, out-of-the-way joints shoehorned into unusual locations. Among those, *atomic is definitely unique...and not just for the asterisk and lower-case lettering in its name.

The cafe sits in a space that once housed a *Calgary Herald* printing press. There's enough room for a small prep area, three tiny tables, and ten stools. Did someone say bathroom? Nope, not here.

But what *atomic lacks in size, it makes up in attitude. Jessica and Russell Bohrson, a powerful sibling duo, have developed a list of atomic-themed drinks that revolve around green or black tea and caramel-tapioca bubbles they call "atomic orbs." And they do yogurt-blended shakes with juices ("yo*atomics") or espresso shakes ("mochatomics"). On the food side, there are the "sub-atomic" sandwiches of spicy satay beef and the inspiration of the day.

The Bohrsons play against their high-priced neighbours in the heart of downtown Calgary by offering a sandwich and a drink for under $10. Not that they think small. They recently put a business plan forward to CBC Television's *Dragons' Den* and convinced the show's high rollers to invest in their expansion. So, look for a second or third *atomic to open soon in Calgary. After that, the mushroom cloud may spread globally.

www.atomicexperience.com

Address
623–1 Street SW

Phone
228·6642

Hours
Monday–Friday
10:30 am–6:30 pm

Reservations
Not accepted

Cards
V, MC, Debit

Drinks
No alcoholic beverages

Takeout
Yes

Outdoor Dining
No

A & A Deli

THERE's a distinctive odour around 20th Avenue and 13th Street NW. That's because most days, the door of A & A Deli is open and the Middle Eastern scent of roasting shawarma wafts outside as the meats slowly spin and sizzle inside.

Jimmy Elrafih, a character if ever there was one, has built the rickety old corner store into a mini-shawarma empire with a dozen upright rotisseries turning at any given time. Need a chicken shawarma dripping with garlic sauce or maybe a little tabbouleh or baklava to brighten your day? At 10 am? No problem. How about beef sliced into a warm pita and layered with pungent pickles? At 10 pm? Sure thing (most days).

A & A is an anomaly, a convenience store that has succeeded in the face of corporate chains. Customers love the odd-ball attitude and friendly service, the good food (and lots of it!), and the reasonable prices. And waiting in line? It's the cheapest comedy routine you'll see. Even though there are no indoor tables, lots of folks hang around after they get their food, just to hear Jimmy entertain the crowds.

And yes, you can get a litre of milk and a bag of chips while you're there. Service is what it's all about.

Address
1401 – 20 Avenue NW

Phone
289·1400

Hours
Monday – Friday
9 am – 10 pm

Saturday
10 am – 10 pm

Sunday
10 am – 8 pm

Reservations
Not accepted

Cards
Cash & debit only
ATM

Drinks
No alcoholic beverages

Takeout
Yes
Delivery

Outdoor Dining
Limited

Aamu | Afghani

Up for a little Afghani food? A mantoo (beef dumpling) perhaps? Maybe a little chalau (cumin-scented lamb stew)? Or just a cruise through a $12 buffet to sample the cuisine?

We haven't seen much Afghani cuisine in Calgary—in fact, Aamu is the first of its kind. And it only opened in 2007. But there's a growing Afghani community here, and usually, when there are immigrants, there are restaurants close behind. (There's a new market too—Shaheen Grocery at 105, 4655 – 54 Avenue NE, 293·0909.)

Aamu is a simple, fifty-seat restaurant with a couple of donair rotisseries and a short buffet. There's also a small menu that includes things like beef tenderloin seekh kebab and chicken karahi, as well as the mantoo and chalau. (All of Aamu's meats, by the way, are halal.) You can expect fairly mild spicing here.

Afghani cuisine varies from region to region, but generally it's not nearly as hot as that of its Pakistani neighbour to the south and does not include the fruity depth of Iranian food to the west. Afghani spicing includes saffron, coriander, cardamom, and black pepper.

Much of the food is done as stews, and at Aamu, as in any Afghani restaurant, you'll find long-grained rice in various forms. There will be a pilau, perhaps flavoured with meat stock. And likely a rice pudding, the ending to any fine Afghani meal.

Address
301, 3132–26 Street NE

Phone
735·1116

Hours
Daily
11 am–8 pm

Reservations
Accepted

Cards
V, MC, Debit

Drinks
No alcoholic beverages

Takeout
Yes

Outdoor Dining
No

Aida's | Lebanese

Y ou can spend a piece of change dining along 4th Street SW, but one place that always leaves my wallet smiling is Aida's.

Aida Abboud has been running her eponymous restaurant since 2000. (It's in the spot that was once home to the original My Marvin's—that's for those who remember the Calgary dining scene in the 1970s.) Aida's is a busy joint because it offers a combination of good food, decent prices, fine vegetarian options, pleasant service, and a prime location. (Why does that have to be so unique?)

Aida's is a terrific option for group functions because it covers a lot of bases. You can order from a bunch of appetizers (hummus, mouhammara, fattoush, tabbouleh, and so on), then delve into main courses, and finish with something sweet. For timid palates, there are chicken kebabs on rice and bowls of lentil soup. For vegans, all the above-mentioned appetizers would work. And for the omnivore, the food is just all-round tasty.

A favourite of mine is Aida's creamy mouhammara, her red pepper, walnut, and pomegranate spread. And her fattoush is a mighty fine salad of crunchy greens and crisp pita chips, tinged with the savoury tang of ground sumac. (And I just love saying fattoush.)

Address
2208–4 Street SW

Phone
541·1189

Hours
Monday
11 am–9 pm

Tuesday–Thursday
11 am–10 pm

Friday & Saturday
11 am–11 pm

Reservations
Recommended

Cards
V, MC, AE, Debit

Drinks
Fully licensed

Takeout
Yes

Outdoor Dining
No

Atlas

PERSIAN cuisine remains unexplored territory for a lot of folks. Although it's a food style that harkens back thousands of years, there are not many Persian restaurants anywhere around North America. Fortunately we have Atlas, a professionally run, fifty-five-seat family restaurant and specialty store.

Atlas produces a broad cross-section of the cuisine, including kebabs of chicken, ground beef, sirloin beef, salmon, and vegetables. They're arranged over saffron-tinged rice or wrapped in pitas. Atlas also serves Persian khoreshts, which can best be described as stews. There's the badenjan of eggplant, sirloin, and tomato. And the karafs of celery, sour plum, and tofu (a vegetarian favourite). Plus the fesenjoon of walnuts, pomegranate, and chicken. All have rich, unique flavours. And note the inclusion of fruit. Ingredients such as pomegranate, plum, lime, and cherry frequently highlight Persian dishes, but rarely make them very sweet. Instead, they add a distinct tartness to the food.

Most dishes remain well under $15, unless you move into some of the larger combo platters. So it's exceptional value for the quality and taste.

You can always find a good cup of tea at Atlas too. Strong, black tea, served in glasses along with cubes of sugar. And a piece of pistachio baklava on the side.

This is a restaurant worth exploring.

www.atlascalgary.com

Address
1000–9 Avenue SW

Phone
230·0990

Hours
Tuesday–Sunday
11:30 am–9 pm

Reservations
Recommended

Cards
V, MC, AE, Debit

Drinks
No alcoholic beverages

Takeout
Yes

Outdoor Dining
No

Avellino's Panini

SOMETIMES all I want is a really good sandwich. Top-quality cold cuts, thick slices of decent cheese, interesting condiments like roasted peppers or pesto spread. All on bread with flavour and crunch and texture. Followed by an espresso pulled by someone who knows how. Or maybe by a cool Orangina or Chinotto on a hot day. When that need hits, one of the key places to head is Avellino's Panini on 14th Street, one block north of 17th Avenue SW.

Named after the Italian hometown of one of the owners, Avellino's serves classic Italian panini—mostly on submarine buns. Those are OK, but if they have it, ask for your sandwich to be made with the pizza dough they get from Fat Tony's. They unfortunately only get enough of that dough for a few sandwiches each day, but it works perfectly in their panini press, making just the right texture of toasted crust.

And try the Ottolina espresso. It's one of the smoothest Italian espressos in the city. (I'm differentiating the lighter Italian espresso from the darker Seattle style common in these parts.)

There is another Avellino's in Sun Life Plaza downtown, but somehow, I'm opposed to paying more for parking than for my lunch. If I'm in the area though…

Address
1602–14 Street SW

Phone
244·9001

Hours
Monday–Friday
9 am–9 pm

Saturday & Sunday
10 am–9 pm

Reservations
Accepted

Cards
V, MC, Debit

Drinks
No alcoholic beverages

Takeout
Yes
Delivery

Outdoor Dining
By spring 2008

Other Location

230, 112–4 Avenue SW
(Sun Life Plaza)
233·0777

Avenue Diner

Contemporary Diner

STEPHEN Avenue is a gauntlet of pricey restaurants. But there are a few that go against the grain by offering a good, creative breakfast or lunch at a reasonable price. Avenue Diner is one of them.

Avenue is a long, narrow space that has a lunch counter lined with old tractor seats. (My agrarian butt aches just looking at them.) About fifty other seats are wedged into the space (at tables, thankfully). On any given day—including weekend brunches—they are full.

Folks are chowing down on whole-grain pancakes with organic maple syrup or a big ol' slab of meat loaf with a savoury bread pudding or even truffled scrambled eggs with grilled portobello mushrooms. Everything's under $15, including the buffalo burger with double-smoked bacon, cheddar, and caramelized onions ($14) and their signature white-cheddar mac and cheese ($13). (OK, the six-ounce New York strip with two eggs is $15 on the nose.)

They run the same breakfast-brunch-lunch menu all day long. With one exception. On weekends, they bake waffles.

This is solid, rich, well-conceived, expertly executed food. Light? No. Lots of butter and salt? You bet. They could charge more for it and, considering the neighbourhood, get away with it. But they don't. So more credit to them.

www.avenuediner.com

Address
105 Stephen Avenue SW

Phone
263·2673

Hours
Monday–Friday
7 am–3 pm

Saturday & Sunday
8 am–3 pm

Reservations
Accepted for groups
of 15 or more

Cards
V, MC, AE, Debit

Drinks
Fully licensed

Takeout
Yes

Outdoor Dining
Patio

Baba Ka Dhaba

Pakistani

BABA Ka Dhaba has come a long way from the days when it was a single table parked in front of an open kitchen inside this 17th Avenue building. There are now three tables, and there's a wall dividing the kitchen from the, ahem, dining room.

In fairness, Baba Ka Dhaba is mostly about takeout, and it's one of the few places in town to put a Pakistani spin on the foods of South Central Asia. The dishes sound the same as in many Northern Indian restaurants—chicken tikka, seekh kebab, butter chicken—but the spicing is subtly different. It's simple and forceful. If you like it hot, it's hot here.

It's also cheap. Most dishes are under $7, with some dals around $4 or $5. At the top end, a tandoori fish is $12, and a ginger- and garlic-marinated lamb chop baked in the tandoor oven is $14. (Still sounds like a bargain.)

And this is good food. The seekh kebab is perhaps the best in town. The mix of meats and spices is well balanced, the tandoori cooking releases much of the fat, and the nan served with it is super. It's not the most sophisticated version of this cuisine, but it doesn't pretend to be.

And there's so much more seating now.

Address
3504–17 Avenue SE

Phone
207·5552

Hours
Daily
11 am–11 pm

Reservations
Not accepted

Cards
V, MC, Debit

Drinks
No alcoholic beverages

Takeout
Yes
Delivery

Outdoor Dining
No

Babylon

Arabian

I have to love a place called Short Pants Plaza. Not just because I enjoy the oddity of the name, but also because I am a confirmed year-round shorts wearer myself. I digress, though.

Short Pants Plaza is home to a few good food spots, including Lloyd's Patty Plus, Village Pita, and the fine little Babylon Food Garden. Babylon is the best option of the three for sit-down dining—it has about thirty-five seats. No hand-held menu, though. You choose from pictures hung over the ordering counter or by pointing at what looks good in the steaming trays.

And what looks good might be a stew of chickpeas and lamb or a mixture of minced and spiced beef. Or a falafel combo platter with five hefty falafels on a plate with some hummus (for $10). Or just a straight-ahead shawarma sandwich of beef or chicken.

The flavours at Babylon speak of the desert and of centuries past. They're traditional ones with items like slowly stewed eggplant, okra, potato, or tomato, perhaps seasoned with cumin, mint, thyme, or saffron. (OK, the potatoes and tomatoes came from the New World a few centuries ago.) Served with rice, the dishes are filling and satisfying.

Especially with a thick Arabic coffee. And maybe wearing a pair of short pants too.

Address
255–28 Street SE
(Short Pants Plaza)

Phone
272·2233

Hours
Monday–Friday
9 am–8 pm

Saturday
9 am–7 pm

Reservations
Not accepted

Cards
V, MC, Debit

Drinks
No alcoholic beverages

Takeout
Yes

Outdoor Dining
No

Barpa Bill's

BEST value meal in Banff? Barpa Bill's, hands-down. Most garlic for your buck in the Bow Valley? Probably Bill's as well.

Bill does no-holds-barred Greek fast food, which is pretty much like regular Greek food without the blue-and-white tablecloths. And it's good stuff. His Greek salad is filled with olives and feta, his hummus is as creamy as they come, and his lamb souvlaki is the best I've had this side of Athens. The pita is exceptional, and he even does a mean hamburger.

The toughest part about Bill's is fighting your way to the counter to order. That, and finding a spare stool to sit at. Bill's is tiny—as in sixteen-seats tiny. And I'm issuing a warning against driving or even walking while eating one of Bill's souvlakis. At the very least, you're risking tzatziki sauce down your shirt.

One other note: Bill only takes cash. But since the biggest ticket on the menu is $9 for the whopping double burger, that shouldn't be too onerous. The lamb souvlaki is still a very reasonable $6.

And my final dining caution for Barpa Bill's still stands after many meals here: If one person eats at Bill's, everyone eats at Bill's. You'll know why once you've bitten into his food.

www.barpabills.com

Address
223 Bear Street
Banff

Phone
762·0377

Hours
Daily
11:30 am–8 pm

Reservations
Not accepted

Cards
Cash only

Drinks
No alcoholic beverages

Takeout
Yes

Outdoor Dining
No

The Bison General Store

IF you're feeling like a fine meal in Banff, one of the better places to check out is The Bison Mountain Bistro. It's good, but it's too pricey to be in this book. The same folks who run it, however, operate a small, mainly takeout store on the ground floor underneath that second-floor restaurant. Here you can find some great sandwiches for under $10.

These are high-toned sangers if ever there were. There's a piri-piri-roasted bison one with appenzeller cheese, horseradish butter, shaved onions, watercress, and oven-dried tomatoes for $9.25 (no extra charge for all those words). There's also prosciutto and mozzarella with fresh tomatoes, arugula, grainy mustard mayonnaise, and crema di balsamico. The sandwiches are built on bread baked in-house from frozen dough. In addition, you'll find items like bison chili, bison-tenderloin soup (they're serious about their bison theme here), and a ream of house-made spreads, mustards, and preserves. And the best selection of cheeses in Banff. Sure, those will add up in a hurry, but you can put together a pretty nice picnic lunch or hotel-room dinner for not-too-much money.

There are a few seats in the store, and they do serve wine and beer—so you can say you've dined at The Bison even if you didn't make it to the main dining room upstairs.

www.thebison.ca

Address
211 Bear Street
(The Bison Courtyard)
Banff

Phone
762·5550

Hours
Tuesday–Friday
11 am–6 pm

Saturday & Sunday
10 am–6 pm

Reservations
Not accepted

Cards
V, MC, AE, Debit

Drinks
Beer & wine only

Takeout
Yes

Outdoor Dining
No

Blackfoot Diner

Diner

EVERY city needs a place to get a hot turkey sandwich at 3 am or pancakes and eggs twenty-four hours a day. A place where the table laminate is worn through and where pie is a course, not just an afterthought. A place where the most expensive item is the $14 New York strip with soup or salad, potatoes, mushrooms, garlic toast, and dessert of the day. Every city needs a Blackfoot Diner.

For over fifty years, the Blackfoot has been serving hearty meals to anyone who stops in. And it's been overseen by the indomitable Edna Taylor since day one. Its location near the Deerfoot-Blackfoot interchange, along the railroad tracks and not far from the Stampede Grounds and many of Calgary's industrial highlights, has ensured a constant stream of truckers and diner devotees ever since. (Having a huge parking lot to accommodate eighteen-wheelers doesn't hurt either.)

The food is straight-ahead diner fare. Lots of hot meat sandwiches, burgers, soups, and non-stop breakfast. The only seafood options are clam chowder and battered shrimp, so stick to the sandwiches, the pies, and, well, anything with bacon on it.

And enjoy the decor, a half-century collection of trucking paraphernalia and diner chic. (Just go. Trust me.) And the service. I love being called "hon" by staff who are among the hardest working and friendliest anywhere.

Address
1840–9 Avenue SE

Phone
265·5964

Hours
Daily
24 hours a day

Reservations
Accepted

Cards
V, MC, AE, Debit

Drinks
Beer & wine only

Takeout
Yes

Outdoor Dining
No

Boca Loca

Mexican

I get more requests about where to find good Mexican food than any other cuisine. Which is not surprising, considering the number of Albertans who vacation in Mexico, our passion for richly flavoured foods, and the general shortage of decent Mexican restaurants around here. But there are some good ones.

I always recommend Boca Loca—first, as a source for Mexican groceries and, second, as a location for a fine burrito lunch. Boca Loca is mostly a grocery store, though. There are two tables in the front to chow down on tamales, empanadas, and key lime pie, but in reality, you are dining in the grocery aisles. Considering the tamales are $4 each ($7 for two), the empanadas are $3 with salsa or guacamole, and the pie is $4 a slice, it's a small price to pay. Because this is excellent food, prepared for real by Renette Kurz and her staff.

The salsas and soups are particularly fine. Whether it's a simple pico de gallo, a sassy mango-chipotle salsa, or a creamy guacamole, the salsas always pique the palate. And the daily soup—posole rojo, chicken tortilla, pinto bean, or whatever it is—is always worth ordering. It might even be enough to carry you through until your next trip south.

Note: The Beltline Boca Loca on 11th Street is now owned independently of the Northmount location and has a line of East African ingredients and lunch dishes, in addition to the Mexican ones.

www.bocalocacalgary.com

Address
777 Northmount Drive NW

Phone
289·2202

Hours
Monday–Friday
10 am–6 pm

Saturday
10 am–5 pm

Reservations
Not accepted

Takeout
Yes

Address
1512 – 11 Street SW

Phone
802·4600

Hours
Monday & Tuesday
10 am–6 pm

Wednesday–Saturday
10 am–7:30 pm

Sunday
noon–6 pm

Reservations
Accepted

Takeout
Yes
Delivery

Common Info

Cards
V, MC, Debit

Drinks
No alcoholic beverages

Outdoor Dining
No

Boccavino

MOST pub-type places serve either a British-style menu à la fish and chips or a North American one with chicken wings. So it's refreshing to find a pub-ish place that serves grilled veal on a bun, lamb kebabs, and pizza that doesn't taste like it came out of a box. Boccavino is such a spot (though it does have those chicken wings).

It is attached to Lina's Italian Market, so it's easy to serve real Italian food—they've got the best products in the back. Their simple penne in tomato sauce with freshly ground parmesan is a subtle, flavourful dish. And that grilled veal is fresh, tender, and served on a decent crusty roll.

Boccavino looks like a lounge or pub with its long bar and loads of televisions. But it actually smells good—especially now that it's non-smoking. Big windows fill the place with light, and an open kitchen gives it a friendly neighbourhood tone.

In truth, a number of the dishes push into the high teens. Scampi in butter and white wine is $18. Veal in a mushroom sauce is $19. But avoid the seafood and pricier veal dishes, and most pastas and pizzas are under $15.

And these are hearty helpings. That veal sandwich is substantial and comes with a big bowl of pasta. For $10! *Bella!*

www.boccavino.com

Address
2220 Centre Street N

Phone
276·2030

Hours
Monday–Thursday
11 am–1 am

Friday & Saturday
11 am–2 am

Sunday
4 pm–midnight

Reservations
Accepted

Cards
V, MC, Debit
ATM

Drinks
Fully licensed
Corkage $10

Takeout
Yes

Outdoor Dining
Patio

Bon Appetit

OCCASIONALLY, I'll find myself in the business-park district along 32nd Avenue NE with hunger pangs. And I really like breakfasts or lunches that don't come from chain restaurants. So I'm pretty happy that Bon Appetit is there and doing what they do.

Bon Appetit is a simple, sixty-seat cafe spread over two rooms. It's nothing fancy: concrete floors, paper napkins, green Arborite tabletops unsullied by linens. The key here is the food. It's good, home-cooked fare of liver and onions, fish and chips, sandwiches, and pizzas. Food that's made on the premises.

Catherine tried a turkey pot pie and thought it was delicious. Flaky pastry, lots of turkey and vegetables, not soupy with too much gravy. And with a side Caesar salad, a good lunch for $10. My clam chowder was excellent. So was my beef dip. The meat was roasted more than I like, but fortunately, it was still tender and juicy. All in all, a memorable sandwich with its nice roll and fine dipping sauce.

We were equally impressed with our dessert, a well-produced Bernard Callebaut chocolate mousse. More than enough for the two of us, topped with its spritz of cream and a strawberry. For $4!

What decade is Bon Appetit in? Whichever one it is, I'll take it.

www.bon-appetit.ca

Address
8, 2915–19 Street NE

Phone
313·1152

Hours
Monday–Friday
7 am–3 pm

Reservations
Accepted

Cards
V, MC, AE, Debit

Drinks
Fully licensed

Takeout
Yes

Outdoor Dining
No

Boogie's Burgers

Burgers

THE small, independent burger bar lives on at Boogie's Burgers. It's closing on forty years in the burger biz, and in all that time, it's only had two owners. It seems like it's had some of the same customers for that period too. Boogie's fans are a loyal lot.

Boogie's simply does a good burger, and here, you really can have it any way you want. A basic burger is $4.40, but you can roll right up to $9.20 for Shawn's Burger of three patties, cheese, bacon, fried egg, onions, ketchup, mustard, relish, lettuce, tomato, and onions. No word as to how many of these nasties Shawn has eaten, or if perhaps this was created in memory of him. There's even a salmon burger and a chicken burger and a veggie burger.

Boogie's does hot dogs and chicken fingers too. It's rumoured someone once asked for a green salad. That talk is unsubstantiated, though. (OK, they have started offering a grilled chicken salad.) But still, folks go to Boogie's for the burgers. And for the friendly staff and the homemade feeling of the thirty-seat place. And for the fries. Can't forget the fries—spicy fries too. And onion rings. They're good. And the milkshakes. Yeah, they're good too.

Address
908 Edmonton Trail NE

Phone
230·7070

Hours
Monday–Friday
11 am–9 pm

Saturday
10 am–8 pm

Reservations
Recommended
on weekends

Cards
Cash & debit only

Drinks
Beer & wine only
Free corkage

Takeout
Yes

Outdoor Dining
4 picnic tables

Bumpy's

Espresso Bar/Cafe

IF all Bumpy's did was pull espresso, they'd deserve a page in this book. They serve one of the best in town, using locally roasted Big Mountain beans and other high-end imports. (I'm declaring a tie between Bumpy's, Phil & Sebastian Coffee Company, and Java Jamboree for best all-around coffee in the area.)

Even if you don't drink coffee, though, you'll enjoy Bumpy's. The look is retro-fifties with pastels and black-and-white photo images. The staff is preternaturally pleasant and attentive. Go once and they may just ask if you want your "regular" when you return. And you will return.

Because there's also food. And it's good. Catherine loves their hot oatmeal. You can choose from about twenty different toppings, and she usually has hers with almonds and blueberries. I like the paninis, the house-made cookies and cakes (there's sometimes carrot cake, which is almost as good as my mother-in-law's), the fresh soups and pillowy muffins, and the ridiculously large selection of dry breakfast cereals.

The place runs like a well-oiled machine. It can be crowded and feel chaotic, but things actually move smoothly. Credit for all this ultimately goes to owners John Evans and Mike Spady, two of the best in the biz.

www.bumpyscafe.com

Address
1040–8 Street SW

Phone
265·0244

Hours
Monday–Friday
6:30 am–4:30 pm

Saturday
7:30 am–4 pm

Reservations
Not accepted

Cards
V, MC, Debit

Drinks
No alcoholic beverages

Takeout
Yes

Outdoor Dining
Patio

Cadence

MOST folks who know Cadence know it for its deep, rich Oso Negro coffee. Cadence is perhaps the only coffee shop in Calgary that brews the Nelson-roasted, organic coffees called Oso Negro. And they do a fine job of it.

But this 21st century diner also offers a list of wraps, burgers, and sandwiches (all with fries and all under $11), plus a daily soup-and-sandwich special for $9.45. They turn out pretty hearty Western-style breakfasts too. Loads of bacon and eggs, French toast, and oatmeal laced with raisins, cinnamon, and brown sugar. Plus house-made desserts, including fresh pie daily.

It all fits with the diner look and the Bowness main-street setting. Cadence has character and attitude and substance to back up the tone. It's not retro because it never left the fifties—this place is more of a throwback. But with better food and coffee and fresher air than its dinerish predecessors.

A couple of notes: Watch out for bike gangs on weekends. As in, gangs of cyclists that drop in and consume the place. And remember, Cadence only takes cash and debit. Plus, Cadence is the only place in this book where you can angle park for free.

www.cadencecoffee.com

Address
6407 Bowness Road NW

Phone
247·9955

Hours
Monday–Friday
7 am–4 pm

Saturday & Sunday
8 am–4 pm

Reservations
Not accepted

Cards
Cash & debit only

Drinks
No alcoholic beverages

Takeout
Yes

Outdoor Dining
No

Central Blends

Coffee House

MOST Fridays mornings you can find me in the lineup for caffeine at Central Blends. Once I finish my restaurant review on CBC Radio, I hightail it over to the West Hillhurst coffee shop for a double espresso (with a shot of hot milk) and a muffin. It might be a bran with blueberry or maybe a fruit mix of some sort (just not the ones with almond extract—I've never liked that stuff). If I'm feeling wild and crazy, maybe I'll opt for a hot cinnamon bun (available Wednesdays and Fridays only) or a slice of banana bread. Sufficiently fortified, I head off to the gym, leaving the crowd of quick drop-ins and leisurely paper-readers behind.

Such is life at Central Blends, a community gathering place as much as a coffee shop. A lot of people come and go quickly. Some, though, linger through lunch, chuffing back turkey-cranberry sandwiches and reading every paper in the place. Others leave for a while, only to return for early dinners of soups and sandwiches. And still others gather in groups in the large back room and hold meetings over coffee and sweets. On really nice days, folks lounge at the outside tables and sip their coffee slowly in the morning sun.

Address
203–19 Street NW

Phone
670·5665

Hours
Monday–Friday
7 am–6 pm

Saturday
8 am–5 pm

Reservations
Accepted for groups
of 10 or more

Cards
Cash & debit only

Drinks
No alcoholic beverages

Takeout
Yes

Outdoor Dining
Patio

China Rose

THERE are buffets, and then there are BUFFETS—places set up for the all-you-can-eat crowd. Because there is an all-you-can-eat crowd that loves to move from behind the wheel of the car to behind a mountain of ginger beef in under thirty seconds. To accommodate that, a good buffet must be well planned for traffic flow, well loaded for capacity, well lit for maximum scope-of-field, and well tended for simple freshness.

China Rose understands BUFFET. When they built their 265-seat restaurant off Memorial Drive over a dozen years ago, they installed a buffet that works. The two main hot buffets are square, creating a smooth flow. The side buffets are well stocked and also easy to approach. And the dessert buffet has at least three flavours of Jell-O. See a lineup in one area, and you can move to another. Lighting is good, and display trays are large enough to carry a moderate amount of product. When it runs low, staff are quick to refill it.

China Rose does both a lunch ($12) and a dinner ($16) buffet of Chinese classics. It's good fare, lots of variety, spiced in the medium range. Ordering off the menu brings an even wider variety and on-demand spicing, but the vast majority of customers go for the buffet.

And why not? It's a BUFFET.

Address
228–28 Street SE

Phone
248·2711

Hours
Monday–Thursday
11 am–10 pm

Friday & Saturday
11 am–11 pm

Sunday
noon–10 pm

Reservations
Recommended

Cards
V, MC, AE, Debit

Drinks
Fully licensed
Corkage $15

Takeout
Yes
Delivery

Outdoor Dining
Patio

Chuckwagon

How many restaurants can you think of that raise their own cattle and then supervise the meat cutting and aging? Aside from some high-end steakhouses, that is. Let's see…I can only come up with that red-barn restaurant in Turner Valley, the Chuckwagon Cafe & Grill.

The Chuckwagon seats forty-two in a Western diner setting—it's got the branding-iron and lonesome-cowboy look. You can sit at the lunch counter or park yourself at a table and sip coffee till the cows come home. (Unless you have to go get those cows, of course.)

They serve big breakfasts of eggs with any combo of bacon, ham, sausages, toast, and hash browns. Add on tortillas or pancakes or French toast or a steak, and you're ready for the day. After 11 am, check out a burger or a steak sandwich or a beef clubhouse, all made from house-grown (or ranch-grown, I suppose) beef from owner Terry Myhre's ranch.

And every few weeks, they offer up a special eggs Benedict made with a four-ounce tenderloin for $17. (Have to use up the tenderloin somehow, and it's usually sold out by 1 pm.) That's kicking up the price point of this book, but everything else on the menu is well below $15.

Address
105 Sunset Boulevard
Turner Valley

Phone
933·0003

Hours
Monday–Friday
8 am–2:30 pm

Saturday & Sunday
8 am–3:30 pm

Reservations
Not accepted

Cards
V, MC, Debit

Drinks
No alcoholic beverages

Takeout
Yes

Outdoor Dining
2 picnic tables

Clay Oven

Indian (Punjabi)

WHILE the residents of the Interpacific Business Park have changed frequently over the past decade, one restaurant has remained constant: Clay Oven.

It's sat at the far end of the strip mall for over ten years, and since I first tried it, I've maintained that it has the best Indian breads in the city. Whether it's a simple nan, chapati, or paratha or an onion kulcha or an aloo paratha, the breads here are great. You could make a meal of them, and given that the aloo paratha is filled with spiced potatoes and peas, some people do.

Others come for the $11 lunch buffet on weekdays, one of the best deals in town. Still others come for a full evening meal and sample the lamb karahi or prawn masala or chicken palak, all under $15.

We like the vegetarian dishes here: the aloo gobi of cauliflower and potatoes, the khumb of spiced mushrooms and potatoes, the malai kofta of mixed vegetables and cheese, and the various dal dishes. Not only are they rich and tasty with the breads, they are all under $11.

We also enjoy the casual family atmosphere of Clay Oven and the friendly service style. It's simple and professional at the same time.

And did I mention the breads?

Address
349, 3132–26 Street NE

Phone
250·2161

Hours
Monday–Friday
11:30 am–2 pm

Monday–Thursday
5 pm–9 pm

Friday & Saturday
5 pm–10 pm

Reservations
Recommended

Cards
V, MC, AE, Debit

Drinks
Fully licensed
Corkage $10.95

Takeout
Yes

Outdoor Dining
No

Color Tinto

Latin & Global

Address
620–12 Avenue SW

Phone
237·6880

Hours
Monday & Friday
7:30 am–6 pm

Tuesday–Thursday
7:30 am–5 pm

Reservations
Accepted

Cards
V, MC, Debit

Drinks
No alcoholic beverages

Takeout
Yes
Delivery

Outdoor Dining
No

I've had a fondness for the restaurant space in the Lorraine Building ever since it was resurrected from a terrible fire a number of years ago. It's a beautiful structure, and the brick-lined, hardwood-floored, sun-washed cafe is a great spot for breakfast or morning coffee. Or midday lunch.

But between the tricky parking in the area and the necessity of being closed weekends and evenings (due to building hour restrictions), many people have never been here. Which has contributed to the demise of more than one restaurant in this space.

Paola Cruz hopes to expel that problem with her Chilean empanadas and Mediterranean sandwiches at Color Tinto. She makes nine different kinds of empanadas, for $8 each, ranging from the tasty Color Verde of salmon, cheese, and spinach to the terrific Tocineta of prunes, bacon, cheese, and rosemary. (Catherine loves the Tocineta; she's always had a thing for the prune-bacon combo.) Cruz also does eclectic meat and vegetable sandwiches, breakfasts of fruits and pastries, and simple desserts of gelato and tiramisu.

She also serves Cafe Feminino coffee, which is produced organically by a Peruvian cooperative of 1,500 women. Plus she offers other fair-trade coffees from the Shuswap Coffee Company. These seem a perfect fit for the smiling owner and the sun-washed, brick-lined, twenty-seven-seat room.

www.colortinto.com

Communitea

SOMETIMES a cafe just feels right, even before you have anything to eat or drink. It has to do with the look, the smell, the energy. Communitea Cafe in Canmore is that kind of spot.

Located in the new Mistaya Place, Communitea is large, seating sixty-five inside and an additional dozen outside. It's bright, with wraparound windows on two sides and a collection of seating that ranges from huge bean bags to wooden chairs.

The menu includes Intelligentsia direct-trade coffee from Chicago and a range of food from shrimp salad rolls and organic spinach salads to beef curry bowls and peanut butter paninis. There are enough organics, meats, sprouts, and brown rice to satisfy carnivores, vegans, and vegetarians of all stripes. Local cookies and biscotti from Sweet Madeira, breads and pastries from Gourmet Croissant, and meats from Valbella are also on the list.

Though sometimes things move a little slow, the staff is a group of smiling, laid-back, "no-worries" folks who make a fine espresso. Communitea's owner, Marnie Dansereau, wants her place to be a community gathering spot, and her plan seems to be working. It's been busy every time I've been there. And that's not just because it's the only place to get a warm Gourmet Croissant pain au chocolat on Sundays when that bakery is closed.

www.thecommunitea.com

Address
117, 1001–6 Avenue
Canmore

Phone
678·6818

Hours
Daily 9 am–5 pm

Reservations
Not accepted

Cards
V, MC, Debit

Drinks
Fully licensed

Takeout
Yes

Outdoor Dining
Small patio

Cravings

THE phrase "something for everyone" is overused. But in the case of Cravings, it describes this restaurant (which is close to Chinook Centre) fairly well. There are sandwiches, pizzas, pastas, rotisserie dishes, chefs' specials, desserts, and coffee. And they are open for breakfast, lunch, and dinner six days a week.

Cravings is operated by GreatEvents, one of Calgary's largest catering outfits. (GreatEvents, for example, handles food services at Spruce Meadows.) So they have a number of staff and production resources to draw upon. (They serve a lot of prime rib at events, so Cravings usually has a beef-and-barley soup. Efficient.)

The look is a "streetscape" of food stations and a sunlit seating area. Choose your food style, step up and order, go sit down, wait for your meal to arrive. If you lean to the big and meaty, you might break the budget, but head for the sandwiches, pastas, or pizzas and you'll be surprised by the combo of quality and price.

Cravings can be confusing the first time or two. You order at each station—a sandwich at one, for instance, a dessert at another. You pay for everything as you leave the restaurant. It's all reasonably quick for a place where most of the fare is prepared to order.

And there does seem to be something for everyone.

www.cravingsmarketrestaurant.com

Address
7207 Fairmount Drive SE

Phone
252·2083

Hours
Monday–Thursday
7 am–9 pm

Friday & Saturday
7 am–10 pm

Reservations
Recommended

Cards
V, MC, AE, Debit

Drinks
Fully licensed
Free corkage

Takeout
Yes

Outdoor Dining
Patio

Crete Souvlaki

Greek

F OLLOWING the time-honoured tradition of "eat here, get gas," Crete Souvlaki serves up calamari and moussaka along with tankfuls of premium unleaded. Pull up to the pumps at the OK gas station on 17th Avenue, west of Crowchild, and you can fill your belly at the same time.

The shopping section of the gas station is packed with the usual chocolate bars (dessert!) and windshield-washer fluids, but it gives way to two small tables plus an even smaller counter set for a cozy couple. This is Crete Souvlaki, identifiable by the tall stack of Styrofoam takeout containers blocking the view of the grill.

The process is simple, though oddly confusing. Step up to the cash register on the gas-station side, order a meal, pay for your food and gas, and take a seat. Or hover in the area if the chairs are occupied. Your food will appear shortly from behind the takeout containers. And keep your eyes peeled. There's no good indication as to whom each container belongs.

But inside, you'll find decent Greek food awaiting you—freshly made, hot, and tasty. Don't expect the best cuts of lamb or the most abundant salads, though. You're not paying a lot after all.

Address
2623–17 Avenue SW

Phone
246·4777

Hours
Monday–Friday
9 am–10:30 pm

Saturday
10 am–10:30 pm

Sunday
2 pm–10 pm

Reservations
Accepted

Cards
V, MC, AE, Debit
ATM

Drinks
No alcoholic beverages

Takeout
Yes
Delivery

Outdoor Dining
No

Dairy Lane | Diner

THE Dairy Lane has been around since 1950. It used to be the Dairy Lane Milk Bar, a little community place where you'd go with your neighbours for ice cream cones and coffee. They'd fry up burgers on the old flat-top grill, churn milkshakes, and scoop up hash browns that had just the right combination of salt and grease.

But like everything else, things change. The original owners are long gone, and it's now the Dairy Lane Cafe. The new proprietors have kept the original metal-trimmed kitchen tables and a chalkboard from the old Model Dairy for daily specials, but they have re-vinyled the chairs and painted the walls in earth tones. The look these days is more retro than authentic diner. And there are now nineteen seats at tables and along a three-chair counter. In summer, there's also a twenty-seat patio out front.

The owners have adopted a breakfast and lunch approach. There are lots of eggs, done omelette-style, over easy, poached, wrapped into burritos with beans, or slid onto English muffins and turned into Benedicts. Burgers and quesadillas and sandwiches are served for lunch. And always, there are the milkshakes in traditional vanilla, chocolate, and strawberry. Nothing cutting edge here, and I think everyone's happy about that.

Address
319–19 Street NW

Phone
283·2497

Hours
Monday–Friday
7 am–3 pm

Saturday & Sunday
8 am–3:30 pm

Reservations
Not accepted

Cards
V, MC, Debit

Drinks
Fully licensed

Takeout
Yes

Outdoor Dining
Patio

Dell Cafe

Chinese & Western

THE Dell Cafe celebrates its 50th anniversary in 2008. That longevity alone merits a page in this book. (Interesting that the Dell's review falls one page behind another old-timer, the Dairy Lane.)

Sure, things have changed a bit since 1958. There are new owners (well, that was at least fifteen years ago). And the prices have gone up. But the Dell is one of the few places still serving that Prairie combo-cuisine known as Chinese and Western. So a group of four can have sweet-and-sour pork, a bacon cheeseburger, liver and onions, and ginger beef, all at the same time. And each for under $10.

The Dell is an eclectic place where this mixed menu works. About fifty chairs are lined up at Arborite-topped tables. The walls are covered in a mishmash of memorabilia from decades past. The kitchen is visible via a pass-through window, and the bathrooms …well, don't expect too much.

Dell connoisseurs order their regular meals and barely have to sit down before they're delivered. (A friend of mine swears by the curried shrimp; another, by the roast turkey.) For non-regulars, it's an easy stroll through a menu filled with Denver omelettes and BLTs. And a trip down memory lane with onion rings and hot beef sandwiches that hit just the right spot.

Address
7930 Bowness Road NW

Phone
288·3606

Hours
Monday–Friday
8 am–7:30 pm

Saturday
8 am–5 pm

Reservations
Not accepted

Cards
V, MC, AE, Debit

Drinks
No alcoholic beverages

Takeout
Yes

Outdoor Dining
No

Diner Deluxe

Contemporary Diner

Is there anyone in Calgary who has not been to Diner Deluxe? Since it opened in late 2001, it has become many folks' favourite location for a good diner meal. The only hindrance to the passion lies in the ability to get a table. It's small and it's popular. Standing in DD's lineup, waiting for breakfast on a Saturday morning, can be gut-pangingly painful.

Still, it's a great place just to look at, with those diner pastels, the chrome-trimmed, Arborite-topped tables, the Plexiglas lunch counter, and all the lamps and posters from the 1950s and 1960s. Even the bathrooms are funky (in a good way).

The look would be almost enough to convert most folks into Diner Deluxe fans. But it's the food that keeps them coming back: buckwheat-muesli pancakes with berries; sourdough French toast with bacon and smoked cheddar; maple-fried oatmeal with lemon curd and vanilla cream; plus eggs Benedict done four ways. And that's just breakfast. How about baked macaroni with sundried tomatoes and white cheddar or veal meat loaf with Dijon-mashed potatoes or a double-smoked pork chop with roasted-apple sauce for lunch or dinner? And always, milkshakes.

Good stuff all around. Big plates, good prices, nice service. Any wonder there's a lineup?

www.cuisineconcepts.ca

Address
804 Edmonton Trail NE

Phone
276·5499

Hours
Monday–Friday
7:30 am–9:30 pm

Saturday
8 am–3 pm
5 pm–9:30 pm

Sunday & Holidays
8 am–3 pm

Reservations
Accepted for dinner
for groups of 7 or more
and for breakfast
Monday–Friday

Cards
V, MC, AE, Debit

Drinks
Fully licensed
Corkage $15
(Free corkage
Wednesday evenings)

Takeout
Yes

Outdoor Dining
Patio

DinoRosa's

PLUMBING the depths of Macleod Trail for lunch can leave one in a state of culinary despair. Chain restaurants occupy most of the prime locations, and the big malls spew forth food-fare grub. Bleaah!

But hidden in an overly discreet corner of Newport Village (across 90th Avenue from the Carriage House Inn) sits a lively little Italian deli and store—DinoRosa's. This is a fine place to pick up pasta and cheese and cold cuts and other Italian essentials for your home cooking.

And while you're doing all that heavy shopping, it's also a great place for a bowl of minestrone, a meatball sandwich, a tiramisu, and an espresso. Because off to the north side of the store, there's a seating area that was a good restaurant in a past life. DinoRosa's doesn't do the full service like its predecessor, but you can order from their kitchen in the deli section and enjoy your lunch at tables surrounded by colourful Italian murals.

There's nothing fancy about DinoRosa's (meals are served on Styrofoam plates), but the quality of food is first rate. It's freshly made by a coterie of friendly Italian ladies who know their stuff. And who will likely urge you to have a little more. It will be hard to resist.

Address
9140 Macleod Trail S
(Newport Village)

Phone
255·6011

Hours
Monday–Friday
9:30 am–5:30 pm

Saturday
9 am–5 pm

Reservations
Not accepted

Cards
V, MC, AE, Debit

Drinks
Beer & wine only

Takeout
Yes

Outdoor Dining
No

eat! eat! in Inglewood

Home Cooking

WHEN the weather turns cold, I want serious sustenance. No frilly, low-fat, contemporary cuisine. I want food from eat! eat! in Inglewood, a restaurant that serves stick-to-your-ribs stuff.

eat! eat! has thirty-five chairs, each draped in a red, yellow, and blue cover. (An expansion planned for 2008 will kick seating up to sixty.) The walls are decorated with original art, and CKUA plays on the stereo.

It's predominantly a breakfast and lunch place with brekkies of omelettes, granola and yogurt, and bacon and eggs and with lunches of lasagna, chili, nachos, and French onion soup. On the weekends, they make eggs Benedict ($9 for the Benny—bargain!).

They are one of the few places that does porridge. My resident porridge maven—Catherine—went for the cooked oats. Not me. In spite of my groats-and-oats surname, I can't stand the stuff. But she liked it.

I ordered the more civilized whole wheat pancakes with maple pecan butter and syrup. Big pancakes, good ten inchers. Thick and sassy. Two of them. No wimpy CBC Stampede breakfast pancakes, these. They were the kind you could patch a tire with. And served with a perfectly fried easy-over egg, I was ready to start the day...after a nap.

Address
1325–9 Avenue SE

Phone
532·1933

Hours
Monday–Friday
7 am–3 pm

Saturday & Sunday
8 am–3 pm

Reservations
Accepted

Cards
V, MC, Debit

Drinks
Fully licensed
Corkage $10

Takeout
Yes

Outdoor Dining
No

Falafel King

Lebanese

THE King is dead! Long live the King! Subjects of the Falafel King slumped into deep mourning when the 1st Street kingdom fell to redevelopment in 2007. Its huge golden crown had been a beacon of fine Lebanese food for over a decade. But by press time for this book, the always-regal Fauzi Salem had secured a new location just around the corner on Stephen Avenue, and it was almost open.

Salem's falafel sandwiches and beef shawarma, along with his fattoush, tabbouleh, hummus, and baba ghanouj, have gained a loyal following with downtown workers. The food in the original kingdom was always fresh and hot and filled with big flavours (read: garlic). It was also one of the most reliable downtown spots for a good lunch under $10.

Salem's falafel are always fine. I'm particularly fond of his kibbeh, the ground-beef and cracked-wheat balls that are seasoned and stuffed with more ground beef and pine nuts. These seem so simple, but they need just the right touch. I also like Salem's fresh juices—orange, apple, carrot, strawberry, mango—whatever is in season. They're a great adjunct to a falafel sandwich.

There is now a second kingdom too, just off 17th Avenue on 10th Street SW. Salem doesn't own it anymore, but new proprietor Gamul Morsy—a prince in the original falafel kingdom—has maintained both the menu and the food quality.

www.falafelking.ca

Address
225 Stephen Avenue SW

Phone
269·5464

Hours
Daily
9 am–9 pm

Reservations
Not accepted

Cards
V, MC, AE, Debit

Drinks
No alcoholic beverages

Takeout
Yes

Outdoor Dining
Patio

Address
1610–10 Street SW

Phone
802·5464

Hours
Sunday–Wednesday
9 am–midnight

Thursday
9 am–2 am

Friday & Saturday
9 am–3 am

Reservations
Not accepted

Cards
V, MC

Drinks
No alcoholic beverages

Takeout
Yes

Outdoor Dining
Small patio

Fat Kee

Chinese

I love the blazing efficiency of Fat Kee, where regulars order their food as they walk to their tables. They'll ask, for example, for a number 4 (a green onion cake, $3) and a number 51 (salt-and-pepper shrimp, $12) while being ushered by one of the speediest servers in the city.

For those who actually need a menu, here's a hint: They're by the door. Grab one on the way in and study it quickly. Be ready. If you don't order on your dash to the table, you'll be asked what you'd like within seconds of sitting.

Thing is, with over a hundred items on the menu, it's not an easy decision for a newbie. There's chicken in black-bean sauce, Szechuan shrimp, beef with oyster sauce, and Shanghai noodles with satay chicken. All under $12. In fact, excluding the seafood dishes, the menu tops out at $9.25.

Delivery is just as swift as ordering. Take a brief trip to the washroom, and you may return to a steaming bowl of noodles on your table. Worse, they may think you've left and seated someone else in your place. (Both have happened to me.)

Now this is not spectacular food. It's expedient, it's cheap, and it's surprisingly good. I've paid more elsewhere for lesser quality. At Fat Kee, you get what you pay for.

Address
3132–26 Street NE

Phone
250·8436

Hours
Monday–Saturday
11 am–10 pm

Holidays
11 am–5 pm

Reservations
Accepted

Cards
V, MC

Drinks
No alcoholic beverages

Takeout
Yes
Delivery

Outdoor Dining
No

Fat Tony's

WHEN Pulcinella took over the space that for decades was the Stromboli Inn, they replaced the huge old pizza ovens with a big, new wood-burning one. And the old, well-seasoned ovens went to Fat Tony's.

Those ovens are still capable of spinning out some fine pizzas: handmade pies with real pizza dough stretched into a medium thickness, topped with a reasonable cover of tomato sauce, decent cheese, and quality toppings. This is traditional Italian pizza that tastes real.

Fat Tony's pizzas start at $14 for a twelve-inch Margherita and zoom up to $21 for a fourteen-inch, all-meat version covered in pepperoni, ham, and Italian sausage. So it's not cheap-cheap. The most value-conscious dishes are the paninis at $7 and $8 and the lasagna at $7. Tony also does cannoli and tiramisu.

Don't expect much for decor at Fat Tony's. There's more space for ovens than for customers—it's mostly takeout. If you do find a spot on their bench or at one of their two tables, you can text message while trying to chuff back a slice of pizza (they are a Wi-Fi hotspot), but that is probably asking for trouble. Still, if you're up for the challenge, or just a good pizza, Fat Tony's might be the place.

Address
1405–11 Street SW

Phone
228·4467

Hours
Monday–Wednesday
11 am–10 pm

Thursday–Saturday
11 am–11 pm

Sunday
4 pm–10 pm

Reservations
Not accepted

Cards
V, MC, Debit

Drinks
No alcoholic beverages

Takeout
Yes
Delivery

Outdoor Dining
No

Flatlands

Prairie Cuisine

I'D include Flatlands Cafe in this book for the name alone. Kudos to partners Brent Robinson and Andrew Blevins for looking at our landscape and incorporating it into the name.

Fortunately, Flatlands is more than a pretty name. They roast big chunks of bison; bake crusty, cheesy scones; build huge pots of hearty soups; and make breakfast every weekday. They whip up big sandwiches—like warm bison dips or roasted peppers with artichoke and brie—and side them with robust salads. Making as many things in-house as they can, sourcing from local producers what they can't (meats from Canmore's Valbella, for example, and breads from Rustic Sourdough), Flatlands' food tastes downright wholesome. It's the kind of place you want to have nearby for an easy lunch or a quick breakfast. Too bad they're only open weekdays.

But Flatlands is hoping the development of nearby condos will mean longer hours (grab that crowd heading home) and maybe even a liquor license (for when you just don't want to go home). They'll likely keep their simple, cafeteria-style look, however, and their understated decor. As good flatlanders, it wouldn't do to become "showy." Better just to do good work and serve good food. 'Tis the way of the Prairies.

www.flatlandscafe.com

Address
100, 550-11 Avenue SW

Phone
265·7144

Hours
Monday–Friday
7 am–3 pm

Reservations
Accepted

Cards
V, MC, Debit

Drinks
No alcoholic beverages

Takeout
Yes

Outdoor Dining
Small patio

Galaxie Diner

IT would be impossible for Brad Myhre to pack any more seats into his tiny Galaxie Diner. Over the years, he's blown out a storeroom in order to wedge in a booth, he's squeezed as many tables as he could into the front window area, and he's brought capacity up to a whopping thirty-two customers. Still, people line up and wait. Even in the coldest weather.

Waiting for coffee and breakfast with the waft of freshly brewed caffeine in the air? And the sight of folks lingering over their pancakes and omelettes? The humanity! Yet on weekend mornings especially, there will be a clot of people gathered in front of the Galaxie.

And there'll likely be another in front of the Belmont Diner in Marda Loop, Galaxie's sister establishment. They might be waiting for eggs Benedict or a meaty Belmont Bleu Burger and their chance to sit on one of Belmont's hard wooden benches.

Customers just like the look, the taste, the smell, and the feel of Myhre's two diners. The food is plentiful and reasonably cheap, and it all comes together to create a fine breakfast or lunch. There are no pretensions. Just a sense of tradition, of times long past, and of good food today.

www.galaxiediner.ca

www.belmontdiner.ca

Galaxie Diner

Address
1413–11 Street SW

Phone
228·0001

Belmont Diner

Address
1, 2008–33 Avenue SW

Phone
242·6782

Common Info

Hours
Monday–Friday
7 am–3 pm

Saturday, Sunday
& Holidays
7 am–4 pm

Reservations
Not accepted

Cards
Cash only

Drinks
No alcoholic beverages

Takeout
Yes

Outdoor Dining
No

Gourmet Croissant

French Bakery Cafe

I used to say I would fly to Paris just for breakfast if I could. I love real French croissants and the crusty bread, smeared with butter and jam, fresh from the oven. With a good cup of coffee. Fortunately, I don't need to travel for hours to get that treat now. I only have to drive to Canmore.

Ifel and Yasmina Costa, and their children Thomas and Clara, are originally from Paris. They moved to the Rockies a few years ago and are producing breads and pastries every bit as good as those in France. And they should be, since Ifel spent years working in Parisian bakeries.

Beyond the luscious pastries is a list of quiches, sandwiches, crepes, and galettes. (Galettes are the savoury, salted, whole wheat cousins of crepes.) These may be filled with ham or bacon or spinach or Nutella or blueberries or scrambled eggs or whatever is in the kitchen. A simple sugared crepe with maple syrup or lemon juice is sublime. A sandwich is a thing of beauty. There are no wasted crumbs at Gourmet Croissant. Every morsel is superb.

Gourmet Croissant also has a comfortable, yet professional, family atmosphere. Local groups hang out here, other restaurants purchase their products to add to their own menus, and special requests (like a batch of the amazing little cakes called financiers) are accommodated. Without having to go all the way to Paris.

Address
1205 Bow Valley Trail
(Rocky Mountain
Professional Centre)
Canmore

Phone
609·4410

Hours
Monday–Saturday
7:30 am–4:30 pm

Reservations
Accepted for groups
of 10 or more

Cards
V, MC, Debit

Drinks
No alcoholic beverages

Takeout
Yes

Outdoor Dining
Small patio

Gunkan
Japanese

I love a nice view whilst dining. I don't quite know what to make, though, of the cemetery vista afforded by Gunkan Sushi House on 4th Street NW. I suppose I should just enjoy the verdant sweep of trees and grasses along with my spicy-tuna-tempura roll and let go of the other connotations.

Even though Gunkan is in an unusual location, it is an effective one. There are not many sushi bars in the area. It's got parking right out front, and it has the bonus of having replaced a not-so-pleasant pub.

The Gunkan group is from Hong Kong via Toronto and opened the space in late 2007 following some renos: new floors, fresh wall hangings, sparkling sushi bar and tables. It's simple, but it works.

And the menu is creative without being excessively expensive. It specializes in sushi rolls: the Golden Dragon (tempura shrimp, flying-fish roe, and avocado, all wrapped in mango, $12); the Red Dragon (exchange the mango for salmon, $11); the Black Dragon (swap the salmon for barbecued eel, $12); the Green Dragon (just the avocado, $8); and many, many, many more, ranging in price from $4 to $14. This is good value. The rolls are big, well presented, and well served. There's other sushi, rice bowls, teppanyaki, and tempura too.

And then there's that view. Real quiet.

Address
3106B-4 Street NW

Phone
454·7619

Hours
Monday–Thursday
11 am–10 pm

Friday & Saturday
11 am–11 pm

Sunday
noon–10 pm

Reservations
Accepted

Cards
V, MC, AE, Debit

Drinks
Fully licensed

Takeout
Yes

Outdoor Dining
No

Harvest

WANNA know where the locals in Canmore go for a good breakfast bowl of granola or a hot soup-and-sandwich lunch for under $10? Harvest.

Just look for the baby bike-trailers and a herd of lounging dogs, step into the wooden interior splashed with butternut-squash-coloured paint, and order up. Try to be nonchalant. The menu is on a big blackboard at the far end of the room. Unless you're just going to point to the chocolate cake or the croissants in the counter out front, you'll need a moment. (In case of panic, just order the lunch special. It'll be a cup of soup and a sandwich.) Smile, pay, grab a glass of water from the table near the entrance. Pull up a wooden bench. (Figuratively. They're attached to the floor.)

Soak up the atmosphere: There's local art on the walls and lots of talk about cross-country ski trails (winter) or hiking excursions (summer) or mountain footwear (year-round). It won't be long before a smiling server, possibly one of Harvest's three owners, delivers your food. Enjoy a grilled cheese sandwich or a chicken club or a Harvest BLT, maybe a flatbread or a soup or the maple granola with yogurt.

Next time, order your usual.

Address
718–10 Street
Canmore

Phone
678·3747

Hours
Monday–Friday
8 am–4 pm

Sunday
10 am–3 pm

Reservations
Not accepted

Cards
V, MC, Debit

Drinks
No alcoholic beverages

Takeout
Yes
Delivery

Outdoor Dining
Patio

Hawkwood Palace

Chinese

I like menus that keep it simple. How many trendy, contemporary restaurants number their dishes? No, they use long descriptions instead, with each ingredient treated reverentially. I suppose if you're dropping $40 or $50 for an entree, though, you want more than just a number.

But at Hawkwood Palace, they have taken the numbering a step further. They declare their food to be both authentic Peking (some might now call it Beijing) and authentic Cantonese. So, each dish gets a letter as well as a number. The P67 is salt-and-pepper shrimp ($13), where the *P* stands for Peking. The C16 is a Cantonese chicken and oyster-sauce dish ($9.25). The *C* is for Cantonese, not chicken. How clever.

Beyond the menu and the pastel tones of Hawkwood Palace, the food is fast, hot, plentiful, and tasty. The spicing is fairly tame, even on the dishes marked with a chili (in addition to those numbers and letters), so if you're going for the burn, look elsewhere. We find that rice and three other dishes give us a huge dinner under $40 (most items are under $10) and loads of leftovers.

We like the service at Hawkwood Palace too. Brisk, professional, pleasant, and accommodating. And able to help us wade through that menu.

Address
555 Hawkwood Boulevard NW

Phone
241·1888

Hours
Monday–Thursday
4 pm–11 pm

Friday & Saturday
4 pm–11:30 pm

Sunday & Holidays
4 pm–10 pm

Reservations
Recommended

Cards
V, MC, AE, Debit

Drinks
Fully licensed
Corkage $10

Takeout
Yes
Delivery

Outdoor Dining
No

High Country Cafe

Country Cuisine

I T's easy to blow by High Country Cafe on your way to Turner Valley or Longview or even the Millarville Farmers' Market. High Country is small, looks like an old gas station, and is just far enough off the road to ignore.

But do so at your own peril. Because you'll miss one of the better breakfasts and raisin pies you're likely to stumble across. And you could forfeit a lovely sunrise too.

High Country seats only twenty inside, so you might have to get cozy with a stranger. A seat is a seat, after all. Especially if we're talking pie. When it's nice out, though, you can sit at a thirty-five-seat patio where gas pumps used to be.

If you like a straight-up bacon-and-egg-style breakfast, this is your place. With a mug of remarkably good coffee. (For $13 on summer weekends, they also do a breakfast buffet under a tent outside.) And topping out at $10, burgers, hamburger steaks, and fish and chips are the sort of fare for lunch.

But don't miss the pie. Made in-house, the crust is rich and flavourful, and the fillings are thick and heavy. And the price? How does $3 for a hearty slab sound? Like 1964?

Address
Corner of
Highways 22 & 549
Millarville

Phone
931·3866

Hours
Tuesday–Sunday
6 am–3 pm

Reservations
Not accepted

Cards
V, MC, Debit

Drinks
No alcoholic beverages

Takeout
Yes

Outdoor Dining
Patio

Higher Ground

FEW places show the evolution of the contemporary coffee house as much as Higher Ground. It started off in 1982 as a tiny community meeting place that served espresso-based drinks and a few biscotti. (Whatever happened to biscotti anyway?) As the neighbourhood grew, it did too. Over time, it expanded into the sprawling space it now occupies, with its long counter-bar, a bevy of comfy chairs and bistro tables, and even a section with free Internet jacks or paid wireless access (but bring your own laptop).

The espresso machine is a lot bigger now, and Higher Ground serves all fair-trade, shade-grown, mostly organic coffees. They've developed a wine, liqueur, and beer list and created a simple menu that spans breakfast, lunch, and dinner. So you can have a breakfast burrito or a yogurt parfait in the morning, maybe a broccoli salad for lunch, and perhaps a smoked turkey or vegetarian sandwich later. The daily soup-and-sandwich special is a good deal at $8. And there's a big display cooler of sweet treats too. The food is nothing complex, but it's sincere, partly organic, and full of social consciousness.

So this is what a contemporary coffee house looks like these days: decent food, good drink, and lots of communication. Wonder what's next?

www.highergroundcafe.ca

Address
1126 Kensington Road NW

Phone
270·3780

Hours
Monday–Thursday
7 am–11 pm

Friday
7 am–midnight

Saturday
8 am–midnight

Sunday
8 am–11 pm

Reservations
Not accepted

Cards
V, MC, AE, Debit

Drinks
Beer, wine, & liqueur only

Takeout
Yes

Outdoor Dining
Patio

The Holy Grill

IT's hard to find a decent hamburger that hasn't been chain-ified. A burger that's grilled just for you, slid into a reasonable bun, and topped with stuff you like. So, The Holy Grill is a breath of fresh air.

Actually, it's a breath of grilled meat. Step inside the small cafe and inhale deeply. Your lungs will be filled with the smoky, oily residue of grilled meat. (Warning: don't bring your vegan friends.) Listen, too, and there'll be the sweet sizzle of burgerdom in your ears and the hot rasp of freshly cut potatoes hitting super-hot oil.

You can lighten up with a bowl of soup or a panini of zucchini, yams, eggplant, and provolone ($6.45), but even then, the zucchini and yams are grilled. You might as well give in and go for a Gourmet Burger with blue cheese and avocado ($6.15) or a Ranch Burger with cheddar and barbecue sauce ($5.95). What the heck—have some sweet-potato chips on the side. Once you've crossed the threshold, there's no going back. You're getting a big calorie hit at The Holy Grill no matter what you order.

But, hey, you're right across the street from Mountain Equipment Co-op. Why not justify that extra "energy" with some new outdoor gear?

Address
827–10 Avenue SW

Phone
261·9759

Hours
Monday–Saturday
10 am–4 pm

Reservations
Accepted for groups
of 8 or more

Cards
V, MC, AE, Debit

Drinks
Beer & wine only

Takeout
Yes
Delivery

Outdoor Dining
No

Il Centro

Italian

SCROUNGING through the light-industrial zone east of Chinook Centre, it's easy to miss Il Centro. In fact, it would be tempting to give the entire area a pass and head to more fruitful dining locations. But then, you'd be deprived of one of Calgary's best Italian cafes.

At lunch, Il Centro is the kind of place to polish off a decent bowl of pasta or soup, a daily special or a small pizza. Relax at one of the tables topped with red-and-white checkered tablecloths and enjoy the Italian hospitality. On Friday and Saturday nights, go with family or friends and take in Il Centro's casual, fluorescent-lit atmosphere and more good food.

Fedele Ricioppo is known as one of the best *pizzaiolos* in Calgary. His crust, sauce, and toppings are all terrific. And working with his family, he cooks and serves fine fare at much less than you'd pay elsewhere. Sure, you can crank up the bill with calamari and gnocchi appetizers and bottles of Tuscan wine—and it's tempting—but you can also fly under the price radar and eat remarkably cheap here. Pastas are mostly under $10 (a full order of gnocchi is $11.50), and pizzas range from $12 to $22 and are worth every cent.

Address
6036–3 Street SW

Phone
258·2294

Hours
Monday–Thursday
11 am–6 pm

Friday & Saturday
10 am–2:30 pm
5 pm–10:30 pm

Reservations
Highly recommended

Cards
V, MC, Debit

Drinks
Fully licensed
Corkage $15

Takeout
Yes

Outdoor Dining
No

Ironwood

YOU gotta love a barkeep (in a less politically correct world, I would have used the word bar*maid*) who can pull a draft beer, re-set the stage lights, mop down six tables, reel off the specials of the day, set out cutlery, and change the music to your taste between courses. That's the way they make 'em at the Ironwood. No muss, no fuss—just good, in-your-face service that rates a 20 percent tip. One presumes this barkeep would be just as capable of hefting unwanted (read: bad-tipping) customers from the premises with ease.

Said barmaid—sorry, bar*keep*—has the advantage of one of the better pub-grub menus for miles around: bowls of chili, coconut-crusted prawns, buffalo burgers with chipotle mayo, and a rare-roasted lamb sandwich with mustard slaw and red-onion marmalade. Good food with pub prices topping out at $16 for jambalaya or fresh halibut and chips. Most dishes land well below that. (The lamb sandwich is $13!)

You can't beat the setting either—a revived Quonset-hut-machine-shop with 150 heavy (read: non-tossable) chairs and a stage for live and lively music. Good food, good beer, good service, good setting. You gotta love the Ironwood.

www.ironwoodstage.ca

Address
1429–9 Avenue SE

Phone
269·5581

Hours
Monday–Friday
11 am–2 am

Saturday
noon–2 am

Sunday
noon–midnight

Reservations
Recommended

Cards
V, MC, AE, Debit

Drinks
Fully licensed
Corkage $15

Takeout
Yes

Outdoor Dining
No

Istanbul

Turkish

FOLLOWING the Istanbul around Calgary has become a bit of a challenge for folks. The restaurant is now in its fourth location, on 4th Street NW kitty-corner from James Fowler High School.

This may seem to be an odd address, but owner Necmettin Ozkan says he likes it. Each school day, students flood his place, scooping up chicken kebabs and lentil soup and eggplant salad. And in the evening, more fans of Ozkan's Turkish cuisine enjoy the free parking out front and the simple setting.

The Istanbul is not a pretty place. A handful of tables and an open kitchen fill the strip-mall space, and the overhead menu consists of text and backlit photos of the food. (Ozkan has never been one to bump up the price of his meals with costly extras.)

He serves a robust lamb kebab, a great Turkish white-bean salad (piyaz), and the Turkish pide, a type of flatbread topped with meats or cheeses or vegetables. (Just don't call it pizza!) And Ozkan is one of the few chefs in town to make his own donair. I'm quite partial to his rice pudding, rich and creamy as it is.

All his food is reasonably priced, with the lamb kebab topping out the menu at $13. Istanbul offers great flavour and value for the price.

Address
4129–4 Street NW

Phone
229·0542

Hours
Monday – Saturday
11 am – 9 pm

Reservations
Recommended

Cards
V, MC, Debit

Drinks
No alcoholic beverages

Takeout
Yes
Delivery

Outdoor Dining
No

Java Jamboree

Espresso Bar/Cafe

SERIOUS coffee lovers will go almost anywhere for their favourite brew. Many Calgarians make the trek to Cochrane, not just for ice cream but for Les and Ottilia Jaworski's joe at Java Jamboree.

From the outside, Java Jamboree looks like any other strip-mall coffee shop. But once you're inside, the first whiff of espresso leads you to believe otherwise. (Even the aroma in the shop shows off the depth and quality of the coffee.) The setting is comfortably cosmopolitan with bistro tables, loungey chairs, subtle lighting, and loads of magazines. And near the back, the espresso is being drawn with charm and professionalism.

Java Jamboree features Josuma and 49th Parallel beans pulled through the latest, greatest espresso machines (a Synesso at the time of writing). Whether it's brewed or pulled, the caffeine is never less than perfect here.

In addition to a fine cuppa, Java Jamboree serves a range of quesadillas (how about a chicken, roasted vegetable, and cheese one?); paninis (or a salmon, artichoke, and caper version?); and cheesecakes (plus a slice of bumbleberry?). That way, you have time to start with an espresso, have a quick bite, then finish off with a second espresso.

At press time for this book, the Jaworskis were putting the finishing touches on a similar Calgary location called Kawa (pronounced ka-va), which will be located halfway between Bumpy's and Caffe Beano. It should become very busy, very quickly and help cut down on the traffic to Cochrane and back.

www.javajamboree.ca

Address
312–5 Avenue W
(Cochrane Towne Square)
Cochrane

Phone
932·6240

Hours
Monday–Friday
7:30 am–9 pm

Saturday
8 am–6 pm

Sunday
9 am–6 pm

Reservations
Not accepted

Cards
V, MC, AE, Debit

Drinks
No alcoholic beverages

Takeout
Yes

Outdoor Dining
Patio

Kawa Espresso Bar

1333–8 Street SW
Calgary
Phone number TBA

JK Bakery

German Bakery Cafe

Looking for a bowl of homemade soup and a big sandwich on bread still warm from the oven? In Canmore? Willing to pay $9.75 for it? That's a very good deal for the quality at JK Bakery.

Walking into this Railway Avenue establishment is like warping into Bavaria. Big bins are filled with fresh breads, and wood-lined display counters are loaded with slices of mocha cake and carrot cake and deep-dish apple pie. The counter is tended by smiling, flour-dusted staff who alternate between serving customers and kneading dough. In a non-stop whirl, they'll whip up egg-salad sandwiches, package your Black Forest cake slices, and load big orders of baguettes into the waiting JK Bakery truck. This is a hard-working bunch.

JK has a substantial wholesale business, so there is a huge bakery behind the service counter. But they have recently moved the counter farther into what once was baking space in order to make more room for their growing lunch trade. And on nice days, there's a little patio out front. So you don't have to drive one-handed while scarfing back a JK doughnut or Nanaimo bar. Take a moment. Enjoy the view, the staff, and the food at JK.

Address
1514 Railway Avenue
Canmore

Phone
678·4232

Hours
Monday–Friday
8 am–5 pm

Saturday
8 am–4 pm

Reservations
Accepted

Cards
V, MC, Debit

Drinks
No alcoholic beverages

Takeout
Yes

Outdoor Dining
Small patio

Jonas' Restaurant

Hungarian

I'VE noticed that prices at Jonas' have been shooting skyward lately. Downtown rents, staff salaries, and food costs have conspired to vault a number of menu items past $10. Some dishes even cost (gasp) 14 bucks! Full dinner portions of cabbage rolls or chicken paprikash or beef stew with egg noodles for $14? Holy mackerel!

I jest, of course. Jonas' is a full-on Hungarian restaurant. And it really is the only one in Calgary. It serves rich, professionally prepared food, and loads of it. My Hungarian friends all speak fondly of Jonas'. "It's just like home," they say. "Except Jonas' paprikash is better."

You won't go wrong with the creamed lentils and sausage (the Thursday night special) or the roast duck with potatoes and red cabbage (the Wednesday night one) either. Or the lush palacsintas, their dessert crepes.

The kitchen is the domain of Janos Jonas, a native of Budapest. He and his wife Rosza ran restaurants there before coming to Calgary in the late 1990s, and they are skilled in the business. Rosza handles the service side with humour and grace. (Eat up! Don't disappoint her!)

And the best value meal? A big bowl of bean goulash soup for $8. That'll fill any hole in your stomach.

www.jonasrestaurant.homestead.com

Address
937–6 Avenue SW

Phone
262·3302

Hours
Tuesday–Friday
11:30 am–2 pm

Tuesday–Thursday
5 pm–9 pm

Friday & Saturday
5 pm–9:30 pm

Reservations
Recommended

Cards
V, MC, AE, Debit

Drinks
Fully licensed
Corkage $12

Takeout
Yes

Outdoor Dining
No

Joycee's

Caribbean

LET'S be clear. We're talking about Joycee's, the Caribbean market by the Petro-Can on the western edge of Bridgeland. It used to be Joy's, but now it's Joycee's. Totally different person. Similar product, though.

Joycee's carries an abundant supply of Caribbean products: pigeon peas, sugar cane, hard dough bread, Irish moss algae, and Ting soda. You can buy your goat meat here—with or without skin. Plus parts of cow—the foot or the skin, for instance—that you won't see in many neighbourhood butcher shops. The room is bright and sun-washed and filled with cheerful, musical voices to go along with the groceries.

You'll also find some fine Caribbean cooking—jerk chicken, brown stew chicken, various patties, and a range of Island curries. The jerk and brown stew have moderate punch and are plated in robust quantities. They're served bone-in, but there's loads of meat on the bone. Most dishes come with rice and peas—perfect for soaking up the sauces—and Joycee adds a little tub of extra stew sauce to the brown stew chicken. Include a pattie or two (imported from Toronto), and you've got a tasty meal.

To take home. Or to eat at one of Joycee's ten seats, hidden behind the groceries. Either way, Joycee's is worth the visit.

Address
5, 630–1 Avenue NE

Phone
234·9940

Hours
Tuesday–Saturday
10 am–6 pm

Reservations
Not accepted

Cards
V, MC, Debit

Drinks
No alcoholic beverages

Takeout
Yes

Outdoor Dining
No

Kaffee Stube

German

THE moment you walk into Edelweiss Village, the pungent scent of sauerkraut hits your nostrils. Which typically elicits one of two responses: a closed-eye smile and a sense of nirvana or a wrinkled-nose frown and the need to escape. At Edelweiss Village, there are many more of the first than the second, this being a market mecca for all culinary things Germanic, like mustards, jams, chocolates, cheeses, and cold cuts. It's also a place for a serious hot lunch at their fifty-seat Kaffee Stube.

Want some rouladen? Slices of beef rolled with bacon and onions? That's $11.25. How about a chicken or pork schnitzel? That's $10.75. Or a frikadelle patty of pork sausage and ground pork and beef with gravy? That's $9.50. All come with potato salad and a choice of red cabbage or sauerkraut. Mmmm, mmmm. Kaffee Stube also serves vegetarian quiche, lasagna, chili, and a soup selection that, on any given day, might include split pea, clam chowder, or beef barley.

Line up at the counter, watch the staff load up the hot trays, and choose what looks good. You're not going away hungry. Especially if you have a slice of torte— perhaps Black Forest or Sachertorte, mocha cream or lemon-apricot. No cabbage on the side. Just the scent in the air.

www.edelweissimports.com

Address
1921–20 Avenue NW
(Edelweiss Village)

Phone
282·6600

Hours
Monday–Wednesday
9:30 am–6:30 pm

Thursday & Friday
9:30 am–7:30 pm

Saturday
9 am–5:30 pm

Reservations
Not accepted

Cards
V, MC, Debit

Drinks
No alcoholic beverages

Takeout
Yes

Outdoor Dining
No

King's Chinese & Western

THERE'S something about a menu that includes both clubhouse sandwiches and sweet-and-sour pork that makes me feel at home. My fondness for this cross-cultural mélange is a result of my Central Alberta upbringing and more than a few meals at places that served "Chinese and Western" food.

King's is a classic of this peculiarly Prairie style. They do big breakfasts of bacon and eggs or French toast or pancakes and such. (Oddly, the most expensive breakfast is a vegetarian omelette at $8.49.) And there's that list of grilled cheese, closed Denver, and clubhouse sandwiches. (What, no hot beef?) Then there are the Chinese selections of grilled dumplings and garlic ribs and barbecued pork chow mein. There's even King's own version of ginger beef.

But King's main claim to fame is its wonton soup. So much so that they go through thousands—yes, thousands—of wontons every day. They serve them up in six different versions of wonton soup, including the basic one ($7), a seafood version ($9.89), and the war wonton ($8.39) that is loaded with noodles, vegetables, barbecued pork, grilled chicken or beef, eight wontons, and broth. Now that's a bowl of soup.

King's has become so popular over the years that they have spawned four Wonton King outlets around town. But the original is the only one with the full Chinese and Western menu.

www.kingsrestaurant.net

Address
104 Meridian Road NE

Phone
272·2332

Hours
Monday–Friday
7 am–4 pm

Saturday & Sunday
8 am–2 pm

Reservations
Not accepted

Cards
V, Debit

Drinks
No alcoholic beverages

Takeout
Yes

Outdoor Dining
No

Wonton King Locations

7070–11 Street SE
(Deerfoot Meadows)
252·6612

7800–30 Street SE
(Foothills Industrial Park)
236·4224

3449–12 Street NE
291·3538

1235–26 Avenue SE
(Crossroads Market)
No phone

Kinjo

Japanese

Whether Kinjo is a "cheap eat" or not mostly depends on your approach to sushi. It's quite possible to slide into a seat at the oval boat bar, slurp a bowl of miso soup, grab a few plates of sushi, and leave feeling satisfied and budget conscious. Or, if you're like some, you can keep pulling plate after plate of scallops and tuna nigiri off the floating boats and pay a tidy sum.

I'm guilty of the latter more than the former, but when I look at Kinjo's price list, I see it's easy to go cheap. If you eat off the boat bar, just watch the colour of the plate on which the sushi sits. Red plates are $2.90, yellow $3.40, green $4.50, blue $6. There are loads of choices at the low-cost end, so don't despair. And owner Peter Kinjo keeps the place so darn busy, the fish is always fresh and tasty.

Kinjo is not the most elegant place, but it may be the most fun. This converted Tim Hortons (I swear you can still smell the donuts) is almost consumed by the crowded boat bar and Peter Kinjo's huge personality. He'll have you singing, dancing, and enjoying sushi (with a few other Japanese treats) like nowhere else.

Address
7101 Macleod Trail S

Phone
255·8998

Hours
Daily
11:30 am – 10 pm

Reservations
Not accepted

Cards
V, MC, AE, Debit

Drinks
Fully licensed
Corkage $10

Takeout
Yes

Outdoor Dining
Patio

Koi | Modern Pan-Asian

I F Koi were a guy, he'd be covered in tattoos and piercings but wearing a great suit. If Koi were a gal, she'd be the shy one from Purchasing who spends her weekends zip-lining.

On the outside, Koi looks almost corporate in its Beltline, office-tower cloak. But underneath that disguise lays a cafe that teams chunks of brie and pear with organic pumpkin seeds and spinach in a passion-fruit-mango-coconut dressing and tops it all with cranberries. (Sound good? It's vegetarian too!) Or it tosses roasted beets with chickpeas, spinach, and red peppers in a lemon-basil vinaigrette or creates rice bowls covered in coconut-curry and Thai-roasted salmon. The rambunctious flavours are often amplified by a socially conscious background of organic ingredients (including the coffee) and local producers.

But Koi is part of the new New Age. They aren't afraid to use meat. The menu includes roasted turkey, Spolumbo sausages, and ham too. And breakfast includes smoked salmon and a plethora of eggs. Omega-3 eggs, that is. Plus, there is a wine and cocktail list that will make any imbiber smile.

So kick back on the cushy banquettes, listen to the esoteric soundtrack, absorb the various art projects on display, enjoy the eclectic cuisine and the reasonable prices—nothing over $15—and consider a tattoo. Or a zip-line weekend.

www.cafekoi.com

Address
1011-1 Street SW

Phone
206·1564

Hours
Monday–Friday
8:30 am–2 pm

Tuesday–Saturday
2 pm–5 pm (coffee only)
5 pm–10 pm

Reservations
Accepted

Cards
V, MC, Debit

Drinks
Fully licensed
Corkage $15

Takeout
Yes

Outdoor Dining
No

Laggan's

Bakery Cafe

Looking for something quick, tasty, filling, and cheap in Lake Louise? You won't do badly to stop in at Laggan's, a Lake Louise landmark.

It's in the Samson Mall, the L-shaped strip mall that's located at the centre of town. Laggan's will be the place with the most activity around it. I've never seen it without lots of customers. It is very busy, a bit confusing, and always warm. Just get in the first line you see and point to something that looks good. (The food that is. Not the person in front of you.)

Laggan's is part morning bakery to load up for the hills and trails, part cafe for soup-and-sandwich lunches, and part coffee shop for afternoon caffeine and scones. I'm particularly fond of whatever is warm and fresh from the oven. It could be a cookie or a muffin or some undefinable baked goodie with lots of fruit on it.

Laggan's also makes a good pit stop if you're passing through the mountain parks. At about two hours west of Calgary, it's perfect for a quick stretch of the legs, a breath of fresh air, and a bathroom break. Not to mention those freshly baked cookies. (Note: There's a public washroom next door to Laggan's for those in a greater hurry.)

Address
Samson Mall
Lake Louise

Phone
522·2017

Hours
July–September:
Daily
6 am–9 pm

October–June:
Daily
6 am–6 pm

Reservations
Not Accepted

Cards
Cash or debit only

Drinks
No alcoholic beverages

Takeout
Yes

Outdoor Dining
Picnic tables behind

Lazy Loaf & Kettle

Canadian Bistro

Since the early nineties, Helen and Mike Labonté have been baking breads and pastries, making sandwiches and soups, and pulling espressos in their Parkdale cafe. It is all tasty, well priced, and home cooked. (I say the latter with some authority, having gone to school with Helen in our hometown of Wetaskiwin.)

For years, I've made my turkey stuffing with the Lazy Loaf's Kettle Bread. It's a dense, house-baked, multi-grain bread that stands up well to my poultry ministrations. It also forms the backdrop for some excellent sandwiches.

Their baking includes fine cinnamon buns and Nanaimo bars and a whole raft of other comfort-style treats. I like that they do not use preservatives and that if any baking is left over, it goes into a discounted "day-old" bin. (Not that there are many leftovers here.)

It seems they're always renovating the place, trying to squeeze in a few more seats or wedging in another oven or mixer. And however large they build it, it's always busy.

By the time you read this, they will also be open in the evenings, something they've wanted to do for years. They will be offering pastas, daily specials, and Mediterranean-inspired appetizers. I'm sure it will be busy then too.

www.lazyloafandkettle.com

Address
8 Parkdale Crescent NW

Phone
270·7810

Hours
Monday–Friday
7 am–10 pm

Saturday & Sunday
8 am–9 pm

Reservations
Accepted for after 5 pm

Cards
V, MC, AE, Debit

Drinks
Fully licensed

Takeout
Yes

Outdoor Dining
Patio

Le Chien Chaud

How très fancy. N'est-ce pas? Le Chien Chaud est un très bon café pour les hot dogs, je pense.

What better way to fancy up the humble tube steak than by hanging a French moniker on it? And serving it up in eleven different styles?

And a veritable United Nations of canines it is. Le Chien Chaud makes a German dog with Oktoberfest mustard and sauerkraut; a Chilean Completo with guacamole and aji sauce; a Chicago version with celery salt and a sport pepper; a Mediterranean one with hummus and artichoke hearts; and even a good-old Canadian dog that you can dress however you like. And, of course, there is a French chien chaud with Dijon mustard and herbes de Provence. All in the $5 range.

To finish off, what could fit better than a Rice Krispie square? Peut-être un San Pellegrino or an Orangina or a good old Coca-Cola?

Eat in, standing up or seated in Le Chien Chaud's tidy and tiny 4th Street space. Or stroll down the street looking in the windows of all the restaurants. And at the patrons who lust after your chien. Try not to look too smug. Especially with mustard on your face.

www.lechienchaud.com

Address
3, 2015–4 Street SW

Phone
229·3641

Hours
May–October:
Monday–Thursday
11 am–8 pm

Friday & Saturday
11 am–9 pm

Sunday
noon–6 pm

November–April:
Monday–Saturday
11 am–8 pm

Sunday
noon–5 pm

Reservations
Accepted

Cards
V, MC, Debit

Drinks
No alcoholic beverages

Takeout
Yes
Delivery

Outdoor Dining
Small patio

Lion's Den | Diner

NEXT time you buzz by the corner of 17th Avenue and Macleod Trail, peer over at the northwest corner. Is the Lion's Den still there? It's quite possible that the little diner that could may have been converted into either a pile of rubble or even an emerging high-rise. But if there's still a neon "open" sign glowing in the window and you have a few minutes and an appetite to spare, pop in.

You could down a classic clubhouse sandwich with some of the best, hottest hand-cut fries in the city. You could spin around on a vinyl-coated twirly stool at the lunch counter and tuck into a milkshake or a slab of pie. Or you could slide into a booth and enjoy the jokes of owner Rico Festa and the food of his charming wife Rose. Perhaps a hot turkey sandwich and a robust bowl of soup (with packaged crackers!) or an excellent slab of house-made lasagna.

Any way you put it, it will be time, money, and appetite well spent. The food is good, wholesome fare, made fresh on-site every day. (The jokes can be a bit staler, but they're part of the appeal.) Don't wait, though. This area of town is rapidly developing, and the Lion's Den won't be around forever.

Address
234–17 Avenue SE

Phone
265·8482

Hours
Daily
9 am–9 pm

Reservations
Accepted

Cards
V, MC, AE

Drinks
Fully licensed

Takeout
Yes

Outdoor Dining
No

Little Chef

IF any place in this book epitomizes the soul of "cheap eats," it's the Little Chef. This unassuming Strathcona restaurant is all about good food, prepared simply and well, priced reasonably, and served in a pleasant, family setting.

No, you won't find any foie gras on the menu, but you will find fish and chips for $10, steak and kidney pie for $11, a hot beef sandwich for $12, and—topping out the list—a New York steak and shrimp combo with vegetables and potatoes for $20. In between, there's a good-sized children's menu (everything, $7); a daily trio combo of soup or salad, sandwich, and dessert for $11.50; a weekend brunch menu with everything under $12; and even a shocking wine list with an organic Chapoutier Rhone red for $30 and an Orvieto for $23.

The Little Chef is skillfully put together too. Owner/chef Arthur Raynor is a former president of the Canadian Federation of Chefs & Cooks, and he knows his business. His meat pies are among the best in the city, and all his food is fresh and tasty. He simply likes having a place that has broad family appeal and where most of his customers are regulars.

By the way, those pies are also available to take home and bake yourself ($7). Just so you can have a little chef in the freezer any time you want.

Address
555 Strathcona Boulevard SW
(Strathcona Square
Shopping Centre)

Phone
242·7219

Hours
Monday–Friday
11 am–8 pm

Saturday & Sunday
9 am–8 pm

Reservations
Recommended

Cards
V, MC, Debit

Drinks
Fully licensed

Takeout
Yes

Outdoor Dining
Patio

Little Italy

Italian

I've been to Little Italy in New York City. I've been to Little Italy in Montreal and Toronto. I've even been to Big Italy, as in that boot-shaped country that dangles into the Mediterranean.

But I had never before been to the littlest Little Italy of all, the twenty-seat cafe in Calgary's South Airways Industrial Park. Until a reader pointed me in its direction, that is. And I'd be willing to bet I'm not alone, South Airways not being a hotbed of any restaurant culture of note. (Although, oddly, there are two entries in this book from that community—the other is Bon Appetit.)

This Little Italy serves spaghetti with meatballs and salami panini and veal cutlet sandwiches to the hungry denizens of the area. They make soups with loads of vegetables and pasta, pull good Italian-style espressos, and always have something sweet for dessert. Their meatball sandwich is pretty good—it's very saucy, but would be all the better if they used a nicer bread.

Service is cafeteria style: Order at the counter and dine with disposable plates and plastic utensils. Floors are linoleum, and the room has all the soul one might imagine from a South Airways cafe. Still, for a hearty lunch in the area for under $10, it's easy enough to deal with.

Address
2, 1935–27 Avenue NE

Phone
291·5654

Hours
Monday–Friday
9 am–4 pm

Reservations
Accepted

Cards
V, MC, Debit

Drinks
No alcoholic beverages

Takeout
Yes
Delivery

Outdoor Dining
No

Luxor

Egyptian

EVER feel like eating a falafel while waiting for the LRT? Maybe you want to buy a tub of tabbouleh to take home? Or down a quick Arabic coffee?

Luxor Emporium & Cafe is perfectly situated by the LRT tracks to satisfy those needs (the 8th Street station is just outside the doors). It can be tempting to race into the cafe, order a kofta (house-made, marinated beef sausage) wrap to-go, and still try to make your train. (Wasn't there a *Seinfeld* episode based on the same concept?) You can be sure that your train mates will sniff out the richness of the Egyptian cuisine you're packing. And probably be tempted to pop in quickly themselves next time.

But it would be more relaxing to dine-in on Luxor's food. The restaurant has forty-five seats, pleasant music, and service as smooth as baba ghannouj. So go, sit back, enjoy an Egyptian pizza (perhaps the King Tut of beef, peppers, and olives, or build your own Tomb Raider with three toppings from a long list of choices), sip a cup of mint tea, maybe nibble a piece of baklava, pick up a few Middle Eastern groceries, and keep an eye on the trains as they pass by. It may not be quite like watching boats drift by on the Nile, but it should still be entertaining. Just don't miss the last one.

Address
937–7 Avenue SW

Phone
282·0030

Hours
Monday–Friday
8 am–10 pm

Saturday
10 am–10 pm

Reservations
Accepted

Cards
V, MC, Debit

Drinks
No alcoholic beverages

Takeout
Yes
Delivery

Outdoor Dining
No

Marv's Diner

IT may not be quite the 1950s inside Marv's Classic Soda Shop, but it's darn close. The racks of Beemans and Black Jack chewing gum, the jars of jawbreakers and stick candy, and the freezer filled with carbonated ice cream all harken back to a different era.

Behind the lunch counter, Marv himself—handlebar moustache perfectly waxed—is pulling sodas and whipping up banana splits and cherry colas. At the drop of a hat, or even the tip of one, Marv will pull over his favourite guitar and wail out an Elvis number or two. Don't be in a hurry for your hot dog or chili-cheese fries; Marv has a large repertoire. Sit back or spin on a twirly vinyl counter stool and enjoy the fifties.

Prices aren't quite what they were back then, but they're pretty good. Sandwiches and burgers—many named after fifties stars like Buddy Holly and James Dean—reach almost $7. (The triple-patty, bacon, and cheese Brutus Burger with fries is a belt-expanding $9). Marv is big on his line of peanut butter burgers, like the Elvis one layered with peanut butter and banana for $5.75—it's a taste treat and a calorie hit all at once! Milkshakes are $4, and malts, $5.35.

But the entertainment is always free.

www.marvsclassics.ca

Address
121 Centre Avenue
Black Diamond

Phone
933·7001

Hours
Wednesday–Monday
11 am–5 pm

Reservations
Accepted

Cards
V, MC, Debit

Drinks
No alcoholic beverages

Takeout
Yes

Outdoor Dining
2 picnic tables

Mediterranean Grill

Middle Eastern

As you whiz by on Macleod Trail, the Mediterranean Grill is easy to dismiss as just another donair shack. But that's a huge mistake. Although the outside (and perhaps, the inside) is nondescript and the address plants it between a cheque-cashing joint and a liquor store, it is one fine little gem of a place.

First, it's very clean. Second, it serves really tasty food. And third, although owner Itzhak Likver calls the Mediterranean Grill a Middle Eastern restaurant, it has a distinctive Israeli spin, probably because Likver hails from Israel. That's a style we don't see a lot of in Calgary. So, the hummus is creamy and less pungent than many of its Lebanese counterparts, the falafel is likewise quite gentle, and the meats exude unique spicing. And by the way, the meats are all halal.

The lamb is particularly notable as being some of the best available anywhere. Fresh Alberta lamb is spiced and marinated for twenty-four hours and then grilled. Plated with hummus, tabbouleh, pickles, rice, onions, lettuce, tomato, cucumber, tzatziki sauce, and pita, it makes for a robust and lush plate of food. And at $11, it's outstanding value.

Whether you eat in or take away, the flavours are big and fresh and the price is right. So, pull in. You'll be happy you did.

Address
108, 6008 Macleod Trail S

Phone
255·0300

Hours
Monday – Saturday
11 am – 7 pm

Reservations
Accepted

Cards
V, MC, Debit

Drinks
No alcoholic beverages

Takeout
Yes

Outdoor Dining
No

Mi Tierra

Mexican Taqueria

I am always on the lookout for a good enchilada, so when I heard there were some to be had in the Latino hotbed of Oakridge, I sprinted right over.

Oakridge?

Hard to believe, but in a sleepy little strip mall, there is a tiny Latin American market with an even smaller taqueria attached to it. And the food in the taqueria is good.

I've had the enchilada verdes—two corn tortillas wrapped around spiced, shredded chicken, topped with salsa verde and cheese, and sided with some refried beans for $8.50. Nicely done. And the beef taco—a pile of rice and shredded beef in a chipotle-tomato sauce on two soft corn tortillas for $3—was great.

But two things about Mi Tierra. First, it's pretty much all takeout. So even though you can sit at a table, your food is served in those difficult Styrofoam containers. And second, what's served is usually only a portion of what the menu says. On any given day, there are things not available. I wanted the enchiladas de mole, but they were out of mole sauce. How is that possible when it's sold in the shop next door?

Regardless, Mi Tierra's food—what there is of it—is good and offers some of the most authentic Mexican flavours north of the Pecos.

Address
2, 10015 Oakfield Drive SW

Phone
238·1749

Hours
Tuesday–Saturday
11:30 am–8 pm

Sunday
noon–5 pm

Reservations
Not accepted

Cards
V, MC, Debit

Drinks
No alcoholic beverages

Takeout
Yes
Delivery

Outdoor Dining
No

Miné | Japanese

EIGHT things about Miné.

First, in spite of its proximity to Canmore's extinct coal mines, it's pronounced mee-nay. That's the nickname of one of the owners.

Second, it's a Japanese restaurant that doesn't serve sushi. They call it Japanese snack-house cuisine, so you'll find a miso broth with pork loin and a tofu dish with grilled eggplant in a hot bean sauce. Or, spreading further into Asia, Thai grilled chicken and Singapore chicken curry.

Third, Miné is good. The food is rich in pungent, savoury flavours. You can get light dishes (sautéed seasonal greens in lemon-ginger-chili vinaigrette) or heavy ones (soy-braised pork belly). Rice bowls or shabu-shabu or salmon cakes served with tartar sauce. Or freshly made ramen noodles.

Fourth, it's in the original long, narrow, twenty-odd-seat Crazyweed location. (Crazyweed fans, fret not; they've relocated to new digs on Railway Avenue. You won't find Crazyweed in this book, though, because it's not "cheap eats" fodder.)

Fifth, pleasant service, great sake list, and upgraded washrooms. Nice.

Sixth, it's still drafty in the winter, thanks to the single door.

Seventh, can't have everything. Just good food at a fine price. (Almost everything is under $15.)

Eighth, remember: It's pronounced mee-nay.

Address
626 Main Street
Canmore

Phone
609·2627

Hours
Thursday—Tuesday
11 am—4 pm
5 pm—close

Reservations
Accepted

Cards
V, MC, Debit

Drinks
Fully licensed

Takeout
Yes

Outdoor Dining
Patio

Mirchi

Pakistani

I T's amazing what can be done with a couple of hundred square feet of real estate. In the tiny space across from the Beltline Safeway, the folks at Mirchi have created a kitchen that fires out a long list of Pakistani foods, a hot table to keep some of them warm, and a seating area for about fifteen. Add in a pop cooler and a washroom, and it can get a little crowded. Especially when customers drop in for their takeout meals.

Mirchi—meaning green chili—does a range of beef and chicken kebabs; a battery of vegetable curries, from spinach to cauliflower with potato; a number of tandoor-roasted meats; and various combos. The most expensive individual items are the marinated goat chops and the prawn karahi, each at $14. It's tempting to choose a sizzling hot kebab served with fresh nan, since kebabs are a major specialty here. But it's faster to select from the hot table—one vegetable and one meat dish with rice or nan for $13. Good food, lots of it, rich spices, great nan.

Mirchi is engagingly stylish and comfortable for a quick bite. I could see the Mirchi concept (and look) working well in a much larger restaurant someday. But for now, it's tiny in size, but big in flavour.

Address
101, 825–12 Avenue SW

Phone
245·3663

Hours
Monday–Thursday
noon–10:30 pm

Friday & Saturday
noon–1 am

Sunday
4 pm–9:30 pm

Reservations
Not accepted

Cards
V, MC, AE, Debit

Drinks
No alcoholic beverages

Takeout
Yes

Outdoor Dining
No

Miss Avril's

Caribbean

FIRST, there was the charming, smiling Sherry. Now, there is the charming, smiling Miss Avril. And still, there is the fine Caribbean food in the Astral Centre on Fairmount Drive.

Miss Avril took over Sherry's Caribbean Food in 2007 when Sherry opened a hair salon a few doors away, and she is continuing the tradition of jerk chicken, curry goat, and oxtail. The look is similar too. It's small, casual, and colourfully Caribbean.

The dinner menu is short (three or four entrees) and changes a little every day: Ackee with salt fish is offered only on Tuesday and Thursday evenings, for instance, and jerk chicken, only on Tuesday and Friday evenings. Lunch is made up of a few Caribbean specialties and whatever captures Miss Avril's spirit from the remains of last night's dinner, plus some Western sandwiches and wraps on the side. Most meals run $8 to $12, with a lunch combo of jerk chicken and brown stew chicken with rice and peas and a pile of mixed (frozen) vegetables—a big bunch of food—for $12.

Although the seasoning is gentle by Caribbean standards, it is by no means weak. All the richness of Caribbean spicing is there. And with an abundance of hot sauces to sparkle it up. The food is quite traditional in the sense that the chicken comes with the bones still in. There's a lot of careful chewing involved in these dishes, but it's worth the effort.

And there's always the bonus of visiting with Miss Avril.

Address
7640 Fairmount Drive SE
(Astral Centre)

Phone
454·2671

Hours
Monday–Friday
10 am–8 pm

Saturday
noon–6 pm

Reservations
Accepted

Cards
V, MC, Debit

Drinks
No alcoholic beverages

Takeout
Yes

Outdoor Dining
No

Mt. Everest's Kitchen

Nepalese

WHEN it comes to Nepalese cuisine, there is only one place to find it in Calgary—Mt. Everest's Kitchen. (Heck, there are only a half-dozen Nepalese restaurants in all of Canada.) Lucky for us, Mt. Everest is very good at what they do.

Nepalese food is a hybrid of Chinese cuisine from the north and Indian from the south, with unique Nepalese herbs and preparations added in. So you'll find momos (steamed dumplings), chatpats (dishes with hot and sour flavours), malas (tandoori-cooked meats on sizzling hot plates), and tarkaris (Nepalese curries). They're all top-quality, but can definitely tally up if you're ordering off the menu.

So in the interest of cheap eating, try their $14 lunch buffet. It is one of the best. The dishes change regularly, so you might find Himalayan ground lamb with chickpeas and vegetable tarkari and Everest chicken (which tastes remarkably like Indian butter chicken). There will always be a dal or two, plus a rice pilau, nan bread, and a tasty dessert like mango rice pudding or mixed fruit in coconut milk. Whatever is there will be hot and fresh.

And you don't have to travel all the way to Kathmandu to find it.

www.everestkitchen.ca

Address
1448A–17 Avenue SW

Phone
806·2337

Hours
Tuesday–Saturday
11:30 am–2 pm

Sunday
noon–2 pm

Sunday &
Tuesday–Thursday
5:30 pm–9:30 pm

Friday & Saturday
5:30 pm–10 pm

Reservations
Recommended

Cards
V, MC, AE, Debit

Drinks
Fully licensed
Corkage $15

Takeout
Yes

Outdoor Dining
No

Niko's Bistro

Italian

EVERY neighbourhood needs a little bistro where you can find a good bowl of pasta, a decent glass of wine, pleasant service, and a comfortable setting. It seems so simple. Why aren't there more?

Hillhurst is fortunate to have Niko's Bistro, a lively forty-five-seat eatery on Kensington Road. It is equally fortunate to have Niko himself, a Croatian expatriate who learned much of his culinary skill in La Brezza's Bridgeland kitchen. His food is simple, robust Italian fare with a touch of Croatian thrown in.

Niko's is the kind of place that offers a daily lunch pasta for $9.50, and that includes Saturdays and Sundays. In truth, it's easy to blow the budget at Niko's—some of the entrees loft into the $20s—but it's still good value for the dollar. And it's easy to go bargain hunting on the menu. Soup of the day is $6, calamari is $8, cannelloni, $12, and spaghettini with smoked salmon, $14.

The room is brightened by photos of Niko's Croatian homeland and softened by red-velour-covered banquettes and chairs. It's cozy yet professional. Staff—including members of Niko's family—readily accommodate customers' needs.

So it's a little bit of Croatia blended with the taste of Italy. That would work in most Calgary neighbourhoods.

www.nikosbistro.ca

Address
1241 Kensington Road NW

Phone
270·0082

Hours
Daily
11 am–2 pm
5 pm–close

Reservations
Recommended

Cards
V, MC, AE, Debit

Drinks
Fully licensed

Takeout
Yes

Outdoor Dining
No

Oishii Village

Japanese

IT was a shame to see the Restaurant Indonesia pass away. For years, it had been the Calgary mainstay of Indonesian cuisine. But I am at least heartened that its replacement—Oishii Village—is doing a good job.

The new owners—two young Japanese women—have scrubbed and repainted and brought the room back to sparkling respectability. Their biggest change has been the addition of a sushi bar in front of the old bar. Considering the popularity of sushi these days and the comparative scarcity of it in this area, that's a smart idea.

Oishii offers some fine bargain lunch combos. For $10, you can choose two items off a list—say sushi and tempura or sashimi and chicken teriyaki—and they come with miso soup and a green salad. A good deal. And the sushi is great. Exact cuts, creative rolls, and a long list of nigiri, maki, cones, and giant rolls. All at reasonable prices, even when not ordering the lunch specials.

Dining-in is popular at Oishii Village, but takeout is even bigger business. Seems Beltliners like their sushi to-go. Service is fast and pleasant too, with the owners handling much of the work. It's great to feel fresh energy in this old place.

Address
1604–14 Street SW

Phone
229·2881

Hours
Monday & Tuesday
11:30 am–2:30 pm
4:30 pm–9:30 pm

Wednesday & Thursday
11:30 am–9:30 pm

Friday
11:30 am–10 pm

Saturday
noon–10 pm

Sunday
noon–9 pm

Reservations
Accepted

Cards
V, MC, AE, Debit

Drinks
Fully licensed
Corkage $7

Takeout
Yes
Delivery

Outdoor Dining
No

Pad Thai | Thai

TROLLING the depths of Banff Avenue for food can be a hit-and-miss operation. There are some good places and some not-so-good places, some pricey ones and some cheap ones. But for flavour, value, and all round yumminess, it's hard to beat the tiny Pad Thai in the Clock Tower Mall.

Pad Thai is so small that almost half of it sits in the hallway of the mall. It's a little Thai joint—just in case you hadn't figured that out—that does a surprising range of curries (red, green, masaman), stir-fries, noodles, soups, and other dishes. Owner/chef Khampiene Gran-Ruaz can crank up the heat to any level you want and make you feel like you're at a Bangkok street market instead of in a Banff basement.

So don't expect a mountainous panorama from Pad Thai. You're not paying for the view and you're not getting one. You're paying for hot, fresh green curry with chicken or for spicy beef in lime juice, chili, and mint. Most dishes are under $10, there's free parking out back, and you're in Banff. Just relax, knock back your pad Thai noodles, and get out into the mountains with a taste of Thailand in your mouth.

Note: Gran-Ruaz and her husband also run the larger and more elaborate Thai Pagoda in Canmore.

Address
110 Banff Avenue
(Clock Tower Mall)
Banff

Phone
762·4911

Hours
Daily
11:30 am–9 pm

Reservations
Accepted for groups
of 6 or more

Cards
V, MC

Drinks
Beer & wine only
Corkage $10

Takeout
Yes

Outdoor Dining
No

Thai Pagoda

1306 Bow Valley Trail
Canmore
609·8090

Palace of Eats

Smoked Meat

THERE is perhaps no place as relentlessly Canadian in this book as the Palace of Eats. Named after a long-gone Calgary food emporium of the past century, this cafe focuses on Montreal smoked meat. Big briskets are steamed and hand-sliced onto Winnipeg rye bread and served with mustard (grown on the Prairies), coleslaw (from good Canadian cabbage), and a kosher dill (also from Montreal). Finishing the plate is a Southern Alberta side dish—Old Dutch potato chips.

A regular smoked meat sandwich filled with six ounces of brisket goes for $9, the eight-ouncer is $11, and the ten-ouncer is $12. You can turn the six-ouncer into a Reuben with Polish sauerkraut and gouda for $11.

You can even eat in at the Palace these days. Initially built as a takeout or stand-at-the-counter spot, the Palace quickly became cognizant of the need for seating. These sandwiches demand your attention and are best eaten sitting down. Not that there is an abundance of places to perch, but at least there are a few.

The Palace of Eats is the sister cafe of the Galaxie Diner next door, so it doesn't feel it has to cover any extra bases. It sticks to what it knows best—smoked meat sandwiches—and it serves them with an East-meets-West panache.

www.palaceofeats.ca

Address
1411–11 Street SW

Phone
244·6602

Hours
Daily
11 am–4 pm

Reservations
Not accepted

Cards
V, MC, Debit

Drinks
No alcoholic beverages

Takeout
Yes

Outdoor Dining
No

Pelican Pier

Seafood

HERE'S one for the good folks in the north who are looking for a decent, friendly, inexpensive seafood joint. Head on over to the intersection of 14th Street and McKnight Boulevard, go just a little farther north on 14th (almost as far as the Winter Club), and you'll find the seaworthy fare of Pelican Pier.

The Pier has been there for a while and has boatloads of fans, but many people drive right by without ever seeing it. Too bad. It's a great alternative for families who want something fresh, quick, versatile, and non-chainish.

They do some fine seafood dishes, especially considering the price. (The Cajun shrimp entree is $15; so is the honey-ginger salmon.) The pastas are always good ($14 to $15), and I can't resist a cup of their seafood chowder for $6 (a big bowl is $10).

But I'm always casting for the fish and chips. Available in haddock, pollock, cod, halibut, or salmon, and ranging from $9 to $14, it's a good feed, especially with the hand-cut fries. And the excellent house-made tartar sauce. Pelican Pier uses high-quality fish and doesn't let it linger, in either the fridge or the fryer. They keep it surprisingly light for something battered and deep-fried. (Note: Lots of things aren't battered and deep-fried here—just whatever *I* order my charming wife points out.)

Address
4404–14 Street NW

Phone
289·6100

Hours
Sunday–Thursday
11:30 am–8:30 pm

Friday & Saturday
11:30 am–9:30 pm

Reservations
Not accepted

Cards
V, MC, Debit

Drinks
Fully licensed

Takeout
Yes

Outdoor Dining
No

Peppino | Italian Deli

As Hillhurst—also known to non-purists as Kensington—gradually evolves, it's comforting to see that some things never change. Like Peppino, which looks almost as it did when it opened in 1993. (In Calgary food terms, that's a looooong time ago.)

The folks who own Peppino call it "Calgary's Littlest Italy," a pretty good handle for the small deli and cafe. Most of the Italian community is further east and north, so Peppino kinda stands out. In a good way.

If you live in the area, this is the place to go for your basic Italian groceries—pasta, olive oil, canned tomatoes, and so on. But it's also a great spot for a quick sandwich, Peppino style. I once took a Joe's Special of mortadella, capicollo, salami, and cheese bathed in roasted-pepper dressing on a plane to Toronto. I thought I was going to have to fend off the other passengers with my plastic fork.

The sandwich varieties are endless: the Italian Perfection, for example, with roast turkey, ham, roast beef and cheese; the Beef Meat Loaf with lean meat loaf, mozzarella, and tomato sauce; and The Hot Italian Meatball with...you guessed it. There are even ten vegetarian choices! All sandwiches are under $8 and are way better than the chain places.

www.peppinogourmet.com

Address
1240 Kensington Road NW

Phone
283·5350

Hours
Monday–Friday
8 am–6 pm

Saturday
10 am–5 pm

Reservations
Not accepted

Cards
V, MC, Debit

Drinks
No alcoholic beverages

Takeout
Yes

Outdoor Dining
Small patio

Pfanntastic Pannenkoek

Dutch Pancakes

I N a pancake-mad town like Calgary, it's not the least bit surprising that the Pfanntastic Pannenkoek Haus has been embraced with open arms...and mouths. Even though Pfanntastic doesn't do fluffy Stampede-style flapjacks, they do over eighty different kinds of flat, twelve-inch, circular delights. In the Dutch tradition.

The batter is somewhere between a Western pancake and a French crepe. So it's fairly thin. But they load it up with bacon and raisins or ham and pineapple or shredded potato and cheese. Or warm blueberries or apples topped with whipped cream and cinnamon. If you can cook it into pancake batter, you'll probably find it here. Any pancake can also be laced with stroop, the thick, molassesy syrup that adds a true taste of Holland.

That is, if you can find the restaurant itself. In spite of its high-traffic location northeast of the confluence of Glenmore and Crowchild Trails, it's buried in a small mall and is almost invisible. But those who have been here know exactly how to manouevre around the area.

And the menu. This is the kind of place where you have a pancake, or pannenkoek, for your main course and another for dessert. A little savoury, a little sweet. Now that's a real Dutch treat.

www.pfanntasticpannenkoek.com

Address
2439−54 Avenue SW

Phone
243·7757

Hours
Wednesday−Friday
10 am−8 pm

Saturday
8 am−8 pm

Sunday
8 am−3 pm

Reservations
Recommended, but not accepted for Saturday before 6 pm or Sunday

Cards
V, MC, AE, Debit

Drinks
Fully licensed

Takeout
Yes

Outdoor Dining
No

Pho Binh Minh

Vietnamese

THERE are loads of places out there that serve a good bowl of Vietnamese bun and a fine pho beef broth, but I've tried to limit the number in this book to a select few.

A couple of Vietnamese friends swear by Pho Binh Minh, a good-sized joint on 17th Avenue SE. It's not much to look at. It's a simple collection of tables and chairs spread over two rooms. (The men's washroom is at the end of a long corridor and has no door.) But Pho Binh Minh faces south, so it's bright and sunny many days.

And it does have one of the best phos (a style of Vietnamese soup) in town. The beef broth is clear and intense, the noodles are fresh and abundant, the green and white onions add a little zip, and the lime and basil heighten each soup's dimension. And that's just to start. You can select your own beef toppings, which range from beef meatballs or satay beef to beef brisket or the always popular (and chewy) tripe. You can even have it with chicken or no meat at all. And the extra large bowls at $7.75 will fill any gullet walking the streets of our fine city.

Address
4710–17 Avenue SE

Phone
235·2521

Hours
Sunday–Thursday
9 am–9 pm

Friday & Saturday
9 am–10 pm

Reservations
Accepted

Cards
V, MC, AE, Debit

Drinks
Beer only
Free corkage

Takeout
Yes
Delivery

Outdoor Dining
No

Pies Plus

FOR over twenty years, the Cousineau family has been pumping out pies. At last count, there were somewhere around a hundred variations in their repertoire, ranging from the eternal favourite (apple) and the always-popular Prizefighter (black and blueberry) to the decadently creamy chocolate-coconut and the simple, seasonal peach.

Many of the pies are available year-round in frozen form, while on a day-to-day basis, there is a smaller selection of fresh-baked whole pies ($17) and pie by the slice ($5). And they are good. Oh, so good.

But what about the "plus" in Pies Plus? That's what they call "light lunches" of soup and salad, salad and quiche, quiche and sandwich, sandwich and soup. You get the idea. Most are combos in the $8 to $12 range, and in my book (the one you're reading, that is), they are more substantial than "light lunches."

Speaking of substantial, Pies Plus bakes a heck of a chicken pot pie. Loads of chicken, lots of vegetables—some still crunchy—and delicate, flaky pastry. A nice piece of work.

The big decision will be whether to side that $9 chicken pie with a $3.60 cup of herbed minestrone soup or a slab of dessert pie covered in a drift of whipped cream. Choosing just one will keep you under my $15 lunch budget. But then again, some days you just have to splurge.

Address
12445 Lake Fraser Drive SE
(Avenida Village)

Phone
271·6616

Hours
Tuesday–Saturday
8 am–6 pm

Reservations
Not accepted

Cards
Cash or cheque only

Drinks
No alcoholic beverages

Takeout
Yes

Outdoor Dining
Patio

Pimento's

Italian

THERE are a ton of dinky restaurants in this book, but none define closet cafe better than these two Pimento's. Together, the Bridgeland and downtown locations are about the size of a decent parking space.

But the trio of Mario Spina, Cosmo Spina, and Joe Capone seems to like confined quarters. They own a mobile pizza oven that is basically a wood-burning oven attached to a van to allow for mobile baking and catering delivery. There's not much room in here either.

The two Pimento's are aimed at different crowds. At the downtown location, where there are three tables, they make a range of fine Italian paninis, sandwiches on crusty rolls, salads, and soup. After that closes at 3 pm, they scoot over to Bridgeland to fire up the pizza oven for the evening trade. Here, where there is only a small corner bench for waiting, they focus on the condo-dwellers— many of whom have had a Pimento panini for lunch—and the takeout pizza biz.

And these are no tawdry pizza pies. They make an excellent crust, mop it down with primo canned Italian tomatoes, and top it with *molto bene* cheeses and cold cuts. The result is a first-rate Italian pizza. One of the most popular is the Pimento's Pizza of tomato, provolone and bocconcino cheeses, and house-made sausage. You don't want to inhale this—it's so tasty, you'll be slowing down to savour it.

The two Pimento's may be tiny, but they think big.

Address
926–5 Avenue SW

Phone
515·0065

Hours
Monday–Friday
10 am–3 pm

Reservations
Not accepted

Cards
Cash & debit only

Drinks
No alcoholic beverages

Takeout
Yes

Outdoor Dining
No

Address
931 General Avenue NE

Phone
515·0075

Hours
Tuesday–Sunday
4 pm–close

Reservations
Not accepted

Cards
V, MC, Debit

Drinks
No alcoholic beverages

Takeout
Yes

Outdoor Dining
No

Prairie Ink | Cafe & Bakery

THERE'S something a bit naughty about having a cup of coffee or a bowl of soup in a bookstore. Many of us were brought up to be reverential about books—to ensure our hands were clean when we touched them and to neither eat nor drink around them. Especially if we hadn't purchased them.

So having lunch at Prairie Ink, surrounded by McNally Robinson's literary tomes, has a doubled-edged benefit. First, it makes us look smart by association. ("Meet me at Prairie Ink—I have to catch up on my Atwood.") Second, it makes us look like devil-may-care adventurers. ("Roasted-tomato soup over a fresh page of prose? Hah! I live on the edge.")

As a bonus, the food is good: decent sandwiches, salads, and soups; breakfast served until 11:30 am (2 pm on Sunday); shade-grown, fair-trade, organic coffees. (We can be socially conscious and intellectual at the same time!)

Prairie Ink also has the advantage of a sun-washed, second-floor setting overlooking Stephen Avenue. It's tranquil and just far enough away from the street buzz. And in summer, the rooftop deck is one of the great hidden treasures of downtown.

So go, enjoy the food and the setting, and pick up a good book on the way out. Maybe even this one.

www.mcnallyrobinson.com

Address
120 Stephen Avenue SW
(McNally Robinson
Booksellers)

Phone
538·1798

Hours
Monday–Wednesday
9:30 am–7 pm

Thursday–Saturday
9:30 am–9 pm

Sunday 11 am–6 pm

Reservations
Accepted for groups
of 6 or more

Cards
V, MC, AE, Debit

Drinks
Fully licensed
Corkage $10

Takeout
Yes

Outdoor Dining
Rooftop Deck

Primal Grounds

PRIMAL Grounds looks like a throwback to a different era. A few decades ago, a place like this would have been filled with long-haired, munchie-driven, patchouli-scented, Pink Floyd-listening VW drivers scarfing down its huge sandwiches, big bowls of soup, and mega slabs of carrot cake. But these days, it's filled with thinner-haired, 10K-racing, condo-living, recycling, Pink Floyd-listening VW drivers. (Hmmm, wonder if they're the same crowd?)

P.G. fits with the greying ponytails. It's an old hamburger stand that was painted and gussied up a bit in the mid-1990s. It's folksy and casual (line up at the counter, order your food, and it somehow finds its way to your table) and oh-so comfortable. It helps that the food is big, mostly house-made, good, and reasonably priced.

They bake their own cracked-rye-molasses bread and use it as the base for their renowned roast turkey sandwich, which comes with lots trimmings, including cranberry sauce. One fine sanger for $7.25. There's always a soup of the day like shrimp and corn chowder ($5) and options that are gluten free. And, of course, the pumpkin-ginger cake, the triple-fudge brownies, the oatmeal-raisin cookies, and the carrot cake with cream cheese icing.

No carrot has died for a worthier cause.

www.primalgrounds.com

Address
3003–37 Street SW

Phone
240·4185

Hours
Monday–Friday
7 am–8 pm

Saturday & Sunday
8 am–6 pm

Reservations
Not accepted

Cards
Cash only

Drinks
No alcoholic beverages

Takeout
Yes
Drive-through window

Outdoor Dining
Patio

Other Location

2000–69 Street SW
(Westside Recreation Centre)
663·0137

Railway Deli

ONCE upon a time, two young brothers named Roland and Harry Griesser toiled in the kitchens of Austria, learning to cut meat and make pies and prepare pâtés and bake thick loaves of bread. One day they decided to move to Canada to work in restaurants. Eventually, armed with very sharp knives, broad shoulders, and Schwarzenegger accents, they settled in Canmore. And after five years operating the eponymous Griesser Spoon, they opened a new place on Railway Avenue.

There are two rooms to their new operation. The deli side is packed with all the cold cuts, condiments, and other take-away goodies you'll need for a weekend in Canmore. And the cafe is the place to go for a quick, high-quality meal. The boys roast chickens, slice prosciutto, and lay out a daily spread accessed via a high-tone cafeteria line. Slide your tray along, design your own sandwich to-go, tuck into a hot schnitzel at one of the fifty-five seats, or lounge over a late-morning breakfast. The food is fast, flavourful, and reasonably priced.

And meaty. The boys love their meat and have created a small side industry for Christmas and Thanksgiving turduckens— the deboned birds (turkeys, ducks, and chickens) stuffed inside each other.

And so goes the tale of the Griesser brothers.

www.railwaydeli.com

Address
702 Bow Valley Trail
Canmore

Phone
678·3637

Hours
Daily
9 am–7 pm

Reservations
Accepted

Cards
V, MC, Debit

Drinks
Fully licensed
Corkage $15

Takeout
Yes
Delivery

Outdoor Dining
Patio

Rincón Latino

Latin American

GOOD Latino food can be hard to find around these parts. But my South American friends swear by Rincón Latino, which is parked out on Glenmore Trail practically beside the Glenmore Inn.

It's run by a fellow from Ecuador, and his menu is a Latin American highlight package of Ecuadorian ceviche, Mexican posole, Colombian arepas, and Venezuelan pabellon. The enchiladas verdes wrapped in corn tortillas are excellent, and the empanaditas are delightful. They even cook the rice different ways to match the varying food cultures. (My only complaint so far is the sangria—they could bump up the quality and intensity of it.)

Aside from authentic preparation, pricing isn't bad. A few dishes slide over $15, but most things are well under. And the plates are filled with food. Then there's the weekday lunch buffet for $10.95. Good deal. And if your appetite and budget allow, try the rice pudding with raisins for $3.95 or the dulce de tres leches cake for $4.95.

Don't expect much for appearance. This used to be a fish and chip shop, and the look hasn't changed much. But the atmosphere is infectious. Even if you don't eat much, Rincón Latino is a good place to visit for the high-energy Latino music and homey feel. You may be up and dancing before you know it.

www.rinconlatino.ca

Address
2770 Glenmore Trail SE

Phone
720·5587

Hours
Tuesday–Friday
11:30 am–9 pm

Saturday
noon–10 pm

Sunday
noon–8 pm

Reservations
Accepted

Cards
V, MC, AE, Debit

Drinks
Fully licensed

Takeout
Yes

Outdoor Dining
No

Rocky's Burgers

SAVE this one for when you're hosting some well-travelled visitors from out of town. Tell them you'll take them out for a fine lunch of Alberta beef. Then slide them over to Rocky's, an old Calgary Transit bus buried hip-deep in Prairie grasses along 12 Street SE.

Park in the gravel lot out front, saunter up to one of the bus's side windows, and order a cheese burger ($4.75) and some fries ($2.75). Ask for the same for your friends, explaining to them that first-timers shouldn't order double burgers. They may protest, but persist. With a smile. Tell them, "No, you're not from around here. Trust me." Keep smiling.

Then wait. Perhaps escort them to one of Rocky's four picnic tables and watch the gophers (pardon me, Richardson's ground squirrels) frolic amidst the fescue. Soak in a little Alberta sun and a touch of automotive exhaust as fellow patrons jockey for parking.

Then retrieve your burgers and fries, maybe add a few milkshakes, and watch as your friends' eyes widen at the size of a single cheese burger. Warn them about the extreme heat of the fresh-cut fries. Then relish in their interjections of delight as their first Rocky burgers slide across their palates. Accept their gratitude and thanks.

And try not to say, "I told you so."

Address
4645–12 Street SE

Phone
243·0405

Hours
Monday–Friday
10 am–3 pm

Reservations
Not accepted
(no seating)

Cards
Cash & debit only

Drinks
No alcoholic beverages

Takeout
Yes

Outdoor Dining
4 picnic tables

The Roti Hut

Caribbean

A good "buss-up-shot" and a "double" can be hard to find around Calgary. We don't have a lot of Caribbean restaurants, and even fewer that specialize in the food of Trinidad and Tobago. Which makes it all the more remarkable that The Roti Hut has been around over fifteen years.

It's a simple place with a small collection of tables and a big menu on the wall. Place your order for roti, along with patties, alu pie, salt fish, or maybe some cow-heel soup, at the counter.

For $4, the house roti consists of curried chicken (bones in) wrapped inside roti dough that has had dal worked into it. You can get a similar preparation but with shrimp or chickpea and potato or boneless meats. Or, you can order a "buss-up-shot." That's roti made without dal, with the meats (chicken or goat) served on the side.

The Roti Hut also serves jerk chicken, brown chicken, pepper shrimp, and the acquired taste of salt fish and ackee. (To some, the cooked fruit called ackee looks like scrambled brain. Mmmm.) All the foods are packed with flavour and are freshly made.

The Roti Hut may not win any design awards, but it always satisfies. And as a postscript: A "double" is a stuffed, fried dumpling.

www.acstown.com/roti

Address
920–36 Street NE

Phone
272·1622

Hours
Daily
9 am–8 pm

Reservations
Accepted

Cards
V, MC, AE, Debit

Drinks
Fully licensed
Corkage $8.95

Takeout
Yes

Outdoor Dining
No

Route 40 Soup Co.

Modern Albertan

Don't go looking for Route 40 on Route 40. You'll find yourself driving through Kananaskis Country getting very peckish. Look in Turner Valley instead. On Main Street.

Route 40 adheres as close as they can to the concept of local, seasonal cuisine. So you'll find wild-sage-roasted Cakadu Heritage lamb and pesto-roasted Bowden Farms chicken along with cinnamon-chipotle-rubbed Alberta flatiron steak. They might be served with Sylvan Star gouda and Paradise Hill greenhouse tomatoes and Chinook honey from Okotoks. Along with some of the most creative soups anywhere. (Ever tried a stinging nettle bisque? Only in the spring, though.)

If this is all sounding expensive, well yeah, it can be pricey. But how about a half-sandwich of tandoori pork with chili and apricot chutney, pickled carrots, grilled pineapple, lime-marinated cabbage, curry mayonnaise, toasted coconut, and peanut-satay-soba noodles? (Yes, all that on one sandwich.) With, a half-bowl (12 ounces) of roasted-tomato-basil soup? For $11.25. Not bad, eh? And that half-sandwich is as big as most full sandwiches you'll find elsewhere.

The only trouble is, filling as it will be, you might want a whole sandwich and some road chips (made from sweet, red, white, and Yukon gold potatoes) and maybe a dessert. Like rum and banana bread pudding with bourbon caramel sauce. That price tag is ticking up. Oh well.

www.route40.ca

Address
146 Main Street
Turner Valley

Phone
933·7676

Hours
Monday–Saturday
11 am–5 pm

Reservations
Recommended

Cards
V, MC, Debit

Drinks
Fully licensed
Corkage $10

Takeout
Yes

Outdoor Dining
Patio

Rustic Sourdough

German Deli

WHEN confronted by sixteen feet of display cooler filled with cold cuts and cheeses, I can be left somewhat speechless. Not without appetite mind you, just without words. Sometimes there's simply too much to choose from.

Such is the case on the deli side of Rustic Sourdough. (On the other side of the wall—the bakery half—there are racks of breads and pastries instead. Even more peril. What's a fella to do?)

If I head into the deli, I am sure to have a sandwich. But choosing from a half-dozen or more breads (all made in their bakery), plus from long lists of meats, cheeses, vegetables, and condiments, I'll either become flummoxed and mute or simply order from the top of the list. And then there is the soup. Given two choices, it usually comes down to eeny, meeny, miny, moe…. Still, roast turkey on multi-grain with havarti, lettuce, tomato, and mayonnaise for $6 is hardly a losing proposition. With a bowl of chicken noodle for an additional $2 (with *two* packets of crackers!), I'm in hog heaven. I might even get lucky enough to snag a seat at one of the four tables.

Rustic Sourdough's deli also carries a full line of German and Eastern European dry goods. And the bakery operates a Friday to Sunday outlet at the Calgary Farmers' Market. No sandwiches there, though.

www.rusticsourdoughbakery.ca

Address
1305–17 Avenue SW

Phone
245·2113

Hours
Monday
10 am–5 pm

Tuesday & Wednesday
8 am–5 pm

Thursday & Friday
8 am–6 pm

Saturday
7 am–5 pm

Reservations
Not accepted

Cards
V, MC, Debit

Drinks
No alcoholic beverages

Takeout
Yes

Outdoor Dining
No

Saigon

Vietnamese

THERE are a number of Vietnamese places in this book that fit the bill of a good-quality noodle house. But, hands down, the spot we have enjoyed the most over the past twenty years—and in two different locations too—is Saigon.

Saigon is more than a Vietnamese noodle house, although it does some of the best pho and bun in the city. Their cha gio rolls wrapped in rice paper are still the best we've had anywhere (believe me, we've been on the lookout). Their lemon-grass chicken is definitive. And the Genghis Khan grill is a fun way to have dinner. You cook your own meats and shrimp on a blazing-hot helmet in Khan-ish fashion; it's a bit pricey for this book, but if you want to splurge a little, it's tasty.

Sticking within our price parameters, though, a bowl of bun is always a fine choice. Most versions here are under $10 and are packed with fresh greens and well-prepared meats.

Saigon is much more about the food than the look. It's an awkward room that has never been well renovated since the departure of the previous Italian tenant about a decade ago. It could use a serious makeover, but as long as the food remains superior, I won't complain too much.

Address
1221–12 Avenue SW

Phone
228·4200

Hours
Monday–Saturday
11 am–10 pm

Reservations
Recommended,
especially on weekends

Cards
V, MC, AE, Debit

Drinks
Fully licensed
Corkage $10

Takeout
Yes

Outdoor Dining
No

Shawarma Station

Lebanese

On a good day, walking along 10th Street north of Memorial Drive provides a cornucopia of delectable scents— Indian tandoori food, Ethiopian stews, roasting coffee, and so on. Strolling by Shawarma Station, the gentle aroma of their spit-roasted chicken and beef wafts out and tempts the nostrils.

Inside, the meats—all halal—are sliced into pitas and doused with your choice of condiments like garlic spread, lettuce, and tomatoes. For $8 to $10. You can pass on the garlic spread if you'd like, but it adds a zip that completes the package. You can accompany your pita wrap with tabbouleh, fattoush, or even Caesar salad. Looking further into the Lebanese menu, there's falafel, kibbeh, baba ghannouj, hummus, and lebneh (strained yogurt) available. It's a surprisingly broad selection for such a small and unassuming place. And it's richly flavoured and true to its culture.

Most people grab something quickly to-go, but others tarry awhile, enjoying their lunch or dinner in the friendly confines of Shawarma Station. Then they can partake of a baklava or rice pudding before venturing back onto the street.

Note: Shawarma Station is one of the more unusual places around in that it has no washroom inside. They have one, but it is outside, down a hall, and behind lock and key. No big deal.

Address
106, 227–10 Street NW

Phone
283·0606

Hours
Daily
9 am–10 pm

Reservations
Accepted

Cards
V, MC, AE, Debit

Drinks
No alcoholic beverages

Takeout
Yes
Delivery

Outdoor Dining
Patio

Shikiji | Japanese

SUSHI is all the craze these days, and there are many good sushi houses around. You can get good sushi at Shikiji too. But I don't actually go there for it. I go to Shikiji for noodles and soup.

Shikiji whips out soba, udon, and ramen noodles by the bucket, ladling them for you into beefy broths and layering them with things like tempura vegetables or barbecued pork. Along the way, you'll be confounded by a table-covering array of sauces and spices and various utensils.

I sometimes go traditional here with the basic buckwheat soba noodles—boiled, cooled, and served with a soy sauce for $8.50. If I'm hungry, I might order the nabeyaki udon, a kind of Japanese hotpot filled with meats, seafood, and vegetables for $13.95. (That's one of the most expensive items on the menu.) Or I might just delve into some ramen (the popular Chinese-influenced wheat noodles) in a soy broth topped with barbecued pork for $11.80. Shikiji also serves the saltier, clear-brothed shio ramen, but that's an acquired taste. Whatever your choice, the noodles and broths are first-rate.

As is the service. Shikiji may be a bargain, but they don't scrimp on style and attention to their customers. This is a pleasant, relaxing restaurant.

www.shikiji.ca

Address
1608 Centre Street N

Phone
520·0093

Hours
Monday–Friday
11:30 am–2:30 pm
5 pm–9 pm

Saturday & Sunday
11:30 am–9 pm

Reservations
Recommended

Cards
V, MC, AE, Debit

Drinks
Fully licensed
Corkage $10

Takeout
Yes

Outdoor Dining
No

Silver Dragon

Chinese

Wᴀɴᴛ a quick, tasty, affordable lunch downtown, but tired of the buffet scene? Dim sum is always an option. And why not try the place that's been doing it the longest? The Silver Dragon has been pushing carts around their Chinatown location for almost forty years.

Most dishes, like salt-and-pepper squid, stuffed peppers, and pork dumplings, are under $4 per basket. Even fancier dishes like black-pepper beef ribs and shrimp-scallop dumplings top out at $5.25. This is good eating. And it's fast. Sure, you may have to wait for the chicken feet and tripe to pass by and hope that the table in front of you doesn't hog all the garlic shrimp, but they keep the trolleys coming.

If you would rather order off the menu, most dishes remain under $12. It's predominantly Cantonese like the dim sum, but some spicier Peking and Szechuan dishes have crept onto it too. Plus there's the great Calgary-Chinese dish of ginger beef.

The toughest part of Silver Dragon dining can be lingering in line on that long stairway while wrestling with the aromas of sesame-tinged wok cooking. That wait can do more damage to the diet—and the budget—than anything.

Address
106–3 Avenue SE
(Second Floor)

Phone
264·5326

Hours
Monday–Thursday
10 am–midnight

Friday & Saturday
9:30 am–2 am

Sunday & Holidays
9:30 am–10:30 pm

Reservations
Recommended, but
only accepted for
Saturday & Sunday
9:30 am–2:30 pm
for groups of 8 or more

Cards
V, MC, AE, Debit

Drinks
Fully licensed
Corkage $7.50

Takeout
Yes
Delivery

Outdoor Dining
No

Other Location

211 Banff Avenue
(Third Floor)
Banff
762·3939

Smokee Lee's

Smoked Meat

Address
Corner of 6 Avenue
& 4 Street SW

Phone
262·2466

Hours
Monday–Friday
10 am–2 pm

Reservations
Not accepted
(no seating)

Cards
V, MC, Debit

Drinks
No alcoholic beverages

Takeout
Yes

Outdoor Dining
1 picnic table

MULLING over the great culinary delights of the world, few can beat standing on a patch of gravel in warm sunlight, sinking your teeth into a warm, thick Montreal smoked meat sandwich. The juices splurting from the sanger and rolling down to your elbows, passersby gawking at the spectacle, the sweet bouquet of smoked meat and car exhaust mingling in your nostrils. The crunch of the dill pickle, the bite of the mustard, the juice continuing to slide and drip. Oh, yeah.

And where does one find this rare *delice?* On the corner of 4th Street and 6th Avenue in the heart of downtown Calgary, at a little wood shack emblazoned with a simple and appropriate name: Smokee Lee's. It sits humbly between sidewalk and parking lot, a meat smoker to one side and the feisty Leslee Matheson holding court inside.

She piles Montreal smoked meat into Winnipeg rye in various weights ranging from four-ounces ($5.50) to seven-ounces ($10.75 for a Reuben). She adds local flavour by smoking her own Alberta AAA round roasts and slicing them into more sandwiches. Everything comes with a choice of mustards, a pickle, and some chips.

Does it get any better than this? Only if you manage to snag at seat at Smokee Lee's single picnic table. On a nice day, that's so fine, it oughtta be illegal.

South Fork

You have to like a place that has Eggs in a Hat on the menu. And Mickey Mouse pancakes. And that makes its own biscuits. Good ones too.

High River's South Fork Restaurant, located on the northern edge of the downtown core, is such a place. It's comfortable and bright and decorated in local Western memorabilia. If you need the washroom, it's outside, around back. Just ask for the key.

Catherine had a hankering for a biscuit, so she ordered one, plus a three-egg omelette with bacon and cheese. It all came with hash browns made in-house, not those frozen ones. The biscuit was everything she had hoped for, and the omelette was even more. It had crisp bacon and real cheddar in every bite. And the price? Seven bucks. Bargain.

I had the hamburger soup, biscuit included, for $3.25. A hearty and tasty bowl. Beefy without being greasy. Then the South Fork Burger, two house-made patties with a slab of ham in between, piled onto a great bun with the usual fixin's. Excellent stuff.

And since that just wasn't enough, we shared a slice of banana-cream pie for dessert. Pleasant, pudding-style filling topped with bananas and whipped cream.

All in, we were out of there for just under $20. And that included the biscuits.

Address
110–1 Street W
High River

Phone
652·3787

Hours
Early March–early November:

Monday–Friday
6 am–3:30 pm

Saturday
6 am–noon

Early November–early March:

Monday–Friday
6 am–3:30 pm

Saturday
7 am–noon

Reservations
Not accepted

Cards
Cash only

Drinks
No alcoholic beverages

Takeout
Yes

Outdoor Dining
Patio

Spolumbo's

I stand in the long line that leads to the ordering counter at Spolumbo's and break into a cold sweat. It's Saturday, so I've already decided on Mama's Meat Loaf on a Bun, a hefty $8 sandwich packed with mortadella and mozzarella. Then I see the sign that says "Homemade Meatballs on a Crusty Bun," and my determination waivers. I love the tomato sauce on the meatballs. But then I smell the gentle sizzle of fresh Italian sausages, and I descend into indecision.

Meat loaf? Meatballs? Italian sausage? The line edges closer, and the time nears for a final answer. I could just take the easy way out and order a thick cold-cut sandwich. What about a salad? Salad? At Spolumbo's? What am I thinking? Breathe.

Maybe a big bowl of soup. I'm dining in today at one of Spolumbo's many tables. No driving. I can have soup! Yes!

But it's Saturday, and they only have meat loaf on Thursdays, Fridays, or Saturdays. I've come full circle. A meat loaf sandwich it is. *With* a bowl of soup! And some fresh chicken-apple sausages to take home for dinner! That covers all the bases.

Except the meatballs. I'll have to come back for the meatballs. Monday…what am I doing Monday?

www.spolumbos.com

Address
1308–9 Avenue SE

Phone
264·6452

Hours
Monday–Saturday
8 am–5:30 pm

Reservations
Accepted for
private room only

Cards
V, MC, AE, Debit

Drinks
Beer & wine only

Takeout
Yes

Outdoor Dining
No

Sushi Hibiki

Japanese

FOR years, Cafe de Tokyo was a lonely outpost of Japanese food in the strip mall at Edmonton Trail and 1st Avenue NE. It was a dowdy little spot with great soup. Eventually, though, the original owner sold, and Cafe de Tokyo morphed into Sushi Hibiki.

The new management did some cosmetic renos, so the place now has a lot of wood trim, no potholes in the linoleum, and nicer bathrooms. The kitchen still consumes almost half the space, and the twenty-odd chairs—new ones, though—continue to rim the room.

Sushi Hibiki does the full sushi menu. But I really wanted a noodle soup, just to see if they were keeping up with the tradition of the place. So I tried the udon served with tempura and three pieces of California roll. To round things out, I also ordered a salmon roll.

The udon bowl had loads of thick noodles, green onions, and shrimp all floating in chicken broth. Good soup. The tempura came on the side: sweet potato, carrot, broccoli, and shrimp. Light tempura crust with a dipping broth. Decent. And both the California and the salmon rolls were great.

Even more impressive was the price. The soup, with the tempura and California roll, was $8.95. With the six-piece salmon roll, I paid just $3 more. And that's a substantial meal.

Sushi Hibiki is no longer a lonely outpost of Japanese cuisine, but it still carries on the fine legacy left by Cafe de Tokyo.

Address
630–1 Avenue NE

Phone
264·1211

Hours
Tuesday–Saturday
11:30 am–2 pm
5 pm–9 pm

Reservations
Recommended

Cards
V, MC, AE, Debit

Drinks
Fully licensed

Takeout
Yes

Outdoor Dining
No

Taketomi Village

Chinese

L AST time I reviewed Taketomi Village, it was Japanese. It still looks the part with its ceramic sake dispenser, wasabi bowls, and Japanese lanterns, but it's not. Now, it's Chinese, even though it has kept its old moniker.

And wading through its broad and lengthy Chinese menu, I notice that it's one of two places in Calgary that serves Hakka cuisine (the other is Karma). Centuries ago, the Hakka people migrated from the Yellow River area of Central China to other Chinese regions and other parts of the world as well. Their cuisine focuses on simple, forceful spicing, seen here in dishes such as the chili chicken and the Manchurian chicken and the Ma Po tofu. Hakka food became hybridized with other cuisines too, so you also see Indian-Hakka items at Taketomi such as curried chicken rolls and paneer pakoras. (There's a big Hakka population in Calcutta.)

The food at Taketomi is cheap. A lunch special of the Manchurian chicken— boneless, battered, and fried—comes with a spring roll and a big scoop of rice for $8. And it packs the heat. As does the hot-and-sour soup. The fare here is also fresh and plentiful; a single dish will not leave you hungry.

So the sushi is long gone, but there are many Chinese options from which to choose, including the milder Cantonese style, the more elaborate Peking, and even good old ginger beef. But try the Hakka. Paneer with spicy garlic sauce is a rare treat.

Address
920 – 36 Street NE

Phone
207 · 8608

Hours
Daily
11:30 am – 1 am

Reservations
Accepted

Cards
V, MC, Debit

Drinks
Fully licensed
Corkage $20

Takeout
Yes
Delivery

Outdoor Dining
No

Tazza

FOR a few years, Tazza has been one of Calgary's most popular Middle Eastern restaurants. It's a quiet, family-run business near the eastern edge of Bridgeland. A little cafe with a dozen or so seats and a rich, fresh menu.

The shawarma (beef), shishtawouk (chicken), and falafel sandwiches, rolled into pita and topped with your choice of condiments, are big sellers here. And they are good. But this kind of sandwich is available in so many places. Where Tazza is different from a lot—aside from the high quality—is in the variety. They have lamb or beef kebab sandwiches, kofta (minced beef) sandwiches, halloumi or labneh cheese sandwiches, and even hummus, baba ghannouj, or tabbouleh sandwiches. They'll wrap almost anything in pita. (Maybe baklava?)

Then there are five kinds of fatayer, the baked pie-like dishes of the Middle East. Plus a half-dozen salads, a bunch of appetizers, and those honey-dripping desserts. And not a one will break the bank.

Most items are prepared for takeout, but you may be lucky enough to get one of Tazza's cafe tables or, in nice weather, a seat on the patio. Either way, it's a pleasant place to spend a few minutes. And a sandwich made the way you want.

Address
1105–1 Avenue NE

Phone
263·5922

Hours
Monday–Friday
10:30 am–8 pm

Saturday
10:30 am–7 pm

Reservations
Not accepted

Cards
V, MC, AE, Debit

Drinks
No alcoholic beverages

Takeout
Yes

Outdoor Dining
Patio

Tiffin

Indian

IN Mumbai, tiffins are a sort of lunch kit delivered to office workers each day. The food that goes inside is usually prepared at home by a spouse, and the tiffins are then delivered through a complex system of cyclists called tiffin-wallas. More simply, though, tiffins are food containers, often made of stainless steel, that can stack together; they are placed in a large, Thermos-like container for insulation until they reach their destinations.

In Calgary, Tiffin is an East-African-influenced Indian restaurant. Step inside and you'll smell the spicy scent of Indian cuisine. You'll also see an odd but fascinating machine, pressing, cooking, and spewing out fresh roti. And these taste pretty good.

You can eat in at Tiffin (they have about fifty seats) on various vegetable or meat curries. Or you can bring your own tiffin to fill and take-away. (You can get the typical Styrofoam take-away containers too.) Some of the uniquely East-African-style dishes here are mogo (fried cassava) and coconut chicken curry.

In the spirit of tiffin, they offer a number of combination dinners, starting with a vegetable curry, rice, and two rotis for $7.50 and ramping up to two meat curries, rice, and three rotis for $12.50. Or make you own selections—but don't forget those warm, tasty rotis.

Address
188–28 Street SE
(Plaza 28)

Phone
273·2420

Hours
Monday–Thursday
11:30 am–8 pm

Friday & Saturday
11:30 am–9 pm

Reservations
Accepted for groups
of 12 or more

Cards
V, MC, AE, Debit

Drinks
Fully licensed

Takeout
Yes
Delivery

Outdoor Dining
No

Tommy Burger Bar

Gourmet Burgers

Address
9629 Macleod Trail S

Phone
258·0668

Hours
Daily
11 am–11 pm

Reservations
Recommended,
especially on weekends

Cards
V, MC, Debit

Drinks
Fully licensed

Takeout
Yes

Outdoor Dining
Patio

WE can argue about whether a place that charges over $10 for a burger belongs in a book on cheap eats. As long as the discussion takes place over one of Tommy Burger's burgers, I'm fine by that.

In the burger scheme of things, Tommy is not cheap. Onion rings are $6, poutine with blue cheese is $8, and Tommy's wings are $10. Even a milkshake is $5. But first, it's all good stuff. And second, even if the burgers are over $10, they are a meal unto themselves. Sure, load up with fries and a shake and you're nearing $20, but that's a lot of food.

Tommy is a by-product of the Metropolitan Grills, those two happening, downtown, after-work hangouts. (Seven, a lively contemporary restaurant and bar, is also part of this group.) The space is a redeveloped Arby's, tarted up in leatherette and blinged with chandeliers and flat screens. And a martini list. It's pretty cool.

And you can have a juicy, house-ground burger topped with maple-pepper bacon or guacamole or prosciutto or sauerkraut or Zinfandel- and thyme-infused onions. They even have salads. (Who are we kidding? Salads? Yeah, right.)

Tommy is a shrine to the meaty gods of burgerdom. Not exactly cheap. But cheap enough.

Trung Nguyen

Vietnamese

IN the world of Vietnamese submarine sandwiches, there are many good ones. I believe the first sub shop in Calgary (and to many palates, still the best in town) was Trung Nguyen, more commonly known as "that little place in that place across from the Harry Hays Building."

That pretty much describes the stand-up kiosk inside the small Chinatown mall on the corner of 1st Street and 3rd Avenue SE. There's been a sub shop there for years, since the dim days when the Vietnamese sub was considered an oddity. (By the way, Vietnamese subs are a remnant of the French Indochina era of freshly grilled meats and vegetables on a baguette.) No one seems clear on exactly how long the Trung Nguyen has been around, though. The current proprietors think they are the fifth or sixth owners.

Nowadays, the Vietnamese chicken satay or pork riblet or veggie subs here are bargain lunch standards. Folks are fond of the filling crunch of Trung Nguyen's crusty bun (I stop short of calling it a baguette); the layers of tangy meats; the crisp lettuce, cilantro, and mint; and the splash of satay sauce. If you want a truly Calgarian spin, try the ginger beef sub. How multicultural can you get? Customers love the prices too. The clubhouse sub is all of $6.50.

So Trung Nguyen, "that little place in that place across from the Harry Hays Building," still comes through. Maybe the first, maybe the best, always a favourite.

Address
10, 132-3 Avenue SE

Phone
266·0728

Hours
Monday–Friday
10 am–6 pm

Saturday & Sunday
11 am–5 pm

Reservations
Not accepted
(no seating)

Cards
Cash only

Drinks
No alcoholic beverages

Takeout
Yes

Outdoor Dining
No

Tubby Dog

A hot dog used to be a sloppy, wet weenie scooped out of a pot of greasy, steaming water and slid into a sawdusty bun. A blob of unnaturally green relish, some yellow mustard, a smear of ketchup, and heaven was on its way. When I was twelve, anyway.

But my tastes have changed (well, somewhat), and hot dogs have gone, if not gourmet, at least "specialized." No one knows this better than Jon Truch, owner of the renowned Tubby Dog.

The Dog is the kind of place you walk past during the day and rarely think of dropping into. But in the weakness of a bleary 2 am, it calls to you. "Have a Slaw Dog," it cajoles, "or a Harlo. It'll be sooo gooood." The siren song continues, "Have you had a PBJ lately? You'll love a dog with peanut butter and jelly. Besides, it's almost breakfast time. We'll break open a fresh box of Cap'n Crunch to make a Cap'ns Dog, just for yooouuu."

Yes, Truch reels us in, one dog at a time. A-Bombs loaded with cheese, bacon, and potato chips; Sumos lined with Japanese mayo, wasabi, and pickled ginger; and Sherm's Ultimate Gripper bacon-wrapped, deep-fried, and topped with more things than I have space for here. You may need to sit awhile on a comfy bench and watch the world go by after this one. It's a gut bomb.

Go. And enjoy. But don't blame me.

Address
103, 1022–17 Avenue SW

Phone
244·0694

Hours
Sunday–Thursday
11:30 am–late

Friday & Saturday
11:30 am–4 am

Reservations
Accepted for groups

Cards
Cash only
ATM

Drinks
Fully licensed
Corkage $5 per person

Takeout
Yes

Outdoor Dining
Big bench

Ukrainian Fine Foods

UKRAINIAN Fine Foods. Some may disparage the name. Fie on them! As someone who grew up in Wetaskiwin and enjoyed the culinary delights of Vegreville, Mundare, and Two Hills, I say the name is fine.

Ukrainian fine, that is—with steaming plates of cabbage rolls, perogies sided with sour cream, and kolbassa; bowls of beet borscht; and slabs of pie. (That's living. A short life maybe, but a tasty one.) It's all packed with Eastern European goodness.

Ukrainian Fine Foods puts out perhaps the most calories per dollar of any place in this book. The above-mentioned plate of two cabbage rolls (big suckers) and six perogies with a big honkin' hunk of kolbassa is $8.45. You can barely carry the plate. All the food is cheap at this twenty-seat cafe. Veal cutlets, baked ham, fried chicken, pork chops, roast turkey—you name it—it's under $10. Each day brings a special, too, and there's always a soup-and-sandwich deal for $6. But save room for pie if you can. A huge wedge of decent strawberry and rhubarb is $2.50!

Sure, Ukrainian Fine Foods is out-of-the-way. And the cinder-block, linoleum-floored space offers little atmosphere. The order-at-the-counter service and Styrofoam plates don't add any either. But still, this is fine food. Ukrainian fine.

Address
540 Cleveland Crescent SE

Phone
287·8884

Hours
Monday–Friday
9 am–3:30 pm

Reservations
Not accepted

Cards
Cash & debit only

Drinks
No alcoholic beverages

Takeout
Yes

Outdoor Dining
1 picnic table

Other Location

1235–26 Avenue SE
(Crossroads Market)
No phone

Uyen Uyen

Vietnamese

IF dowdy and plain are indicators of a good Vietnamese restaurant, then the thirty-one-seat Uyen Uyen should be one fine place. Tucked into a nondescript strip mall on a particularly dour stretch of 16th Avenue, it's easy to miss. Especially if you're distracted by all the activity at Peters' Drive-In a short distance away.

But look a little closer and you'll find a simple, good, and blissfully affordable joint. Uyen Uyen (*uyen* refers to a type of bird) does the full Vietnamese package of vermicelli dishes (called bun), beef noodle soups (pho), and submarine sandwiches (banh mi).

I've had the priciest item on the menu—the stir-fried prawns, beef, and chicken in lemon grass, all heaped on vermicelli for $9.50. It's a lot of food. Good quality and tasty too. Ditto for the shrimp salad rolls. And the folks at Uyen Uyen are particularly proud of their beef curry soup and their grilled chicken with star anise on vermicelli. Perhaps next time.

Service is brisk and friendly—you can be in and out in less than half an hour. So if you need a quick lunch stop on the way through town or if you're in the area, Uyen Uyen makes a pleasant, efficient stop.

Address
420–16 Avenue NE

Phone
276·4800

Hours
Daily
11 am–10 pm

Reservations
Accepted

Cards
V, MC, Debit

Drinks
No alcoholic beverages

Takeout
Yes
Delivery

Outdoor Dining
No

Valbella Cafe

European Deli

THE word "Valbella" pops up in a lot of my writing. For over thirty years, Walter von Rotz and his team at Valbella have been producing outstanding meats, from their bündnerfleisch (air-dried beef) and smoked-peppered duck breast to their Moroccan lamb sausage and veal bratwurst. And, of course, their wide range of cured sausages (the smoked chorizo is amazing). These meats appear on many menus around our area, and the Valbella Deli itself is a meat-lover's mecca.

The deli is required shopping for anyone spending a few days or more in the mountains—it's the place to go for both cured as well as fresh meats, plus salads and breads and condiments. The location in the Elk Run Industrial Park is a little tricky to find, but roll down your car window and follow the sweet smell of smoking meat.

And if you want a quick hit of Valbella goodness right now, you can grab a seat at the cafe attached to the deli. Here you can have a fresh, thick sandwich of Valbella cold cuts and a bowl of soup for under $10. Or a hearty meat pie and a house-baked cookie. They keep the menu simple and meaty. And everything is available for take-away. Not that Valbella products travel very far. They're way too tempting for that.

www.valbellagourmetfoods.ca

Address
104 Elk Run Boulevard
Canmore

Phone
678·4109

Hours
Monday–Friday
8 am–6 pm

Saturday
9 am–5 pm

Reservations
Not accepted

Cards
V, MC, Debit

Drinks
No alcoholic beverages

Takeout
Yes

Outdoor Dining
2 picnic tables

Village Pita

THE area around 28th Street and Memorial Drive SE is fertile ground for inexpensive and multicultural eating. One of my favourites, for its simple approach to fresh, robust Middle Eastern food, is Village Pita.

Stroll in, step up to the counter, read the short overhead menu—unless, like many regulars, you know it by heart—and order. Leave or sit at one of four stools with your hot, hot stuffed pita rolled up in paper. For $3 or $4, you can't beat the quality. And the relentless efficiency of the place.

The owners work long hours at Village Pita. And they produce much of the pita bread we see in other, fancier places. But go to the source and you'll have it steaming from the oven, coated in spinach and feta or topped with beef or the always-popular zataar (a mixture that, here, is thyme, oregano, sumac, and sesame seeds). Purported to enliven the mind and strengthen the body, the zataar pita is popular with students at exam time. It's also a big hit of green herbs for only $2.25.

All of Village Pita's meats are halal, and they are fully stocked with Middle Eastern groceries and sweets. Plus a bag or two of fresh pita to take home.

Address
255–28 Street SE

Phone
273·0330

Hours
Monday–Saturday
8 am–7 pm

Sunday
8:30 am–5 pm

Reservations
Not accepted

Cards
Cash & debit only

Drinks
No alcoholic beverages

Takeout
Yes

Outdoor Dining
No

Vogglio D'Pizza

Pizza

PRUNE and bacon would not usually be my first choice for pizza toppings. And I wouldn't have thought of topping a pie with guava paste or tortilla chips or even kernels of corn. But then, I'd never had a Colombian-style pizza before Vogglio D'Pizza arrived on the scene in the summer of 2007.

Luis Leal worked in and owned pizza parlours in Bogota for fifteen years, so he knows how to toss a primo crust. The dough is handmade daily, and Leal will roll it out to any thickness (thin, regular, or thick) and any size you'd like. He even does it in whole wheat if you want your pizza healthier. Leal also makes the tomato sauce in-house and selects high-quality toppings. Prices range from $5.49 for an individual pizza to almost $28 for an extra-large with just about everything. (If you're not into pizza, he has wings, salads, and a handful of pastas. But you might want to try the Fruit Festival pizza of apple, pineapple, peach, cherry, pear, and prune— he says it's huge in Colombia.)

You can chow down at the counter, but Vogglio is pretty much for take-away. And don't expect posh decor. Leal is putting all his effort into the pizza and is fixing up the front end when time and budget permit. That's OK by me. This kind of quality is its own reward.

Address
1514–14 Street SW

Phone
228·1228
228·1285

Hours
Daily
11:30 am – midnight

Reservations
Not accepted

Cards
V, MC, Debit

Drinks
No alcoholic beverages

Takeout
Yes
Delivery

Outdoor Dining
No

The Wicked Wedge

Pizza

PIZZA doesn't typically improve with age. (Granted, some think the mark of a top-notch pie is how good it tastes for breakfast the next day, but really, it's best fresh out of the oven.) So it's great to see that the twelve-year-old pizzeria known as The Wicked Wedge has gotten better over the years.

The place looks sharp thanks to a fresh paint job, upgraded flooring, new seating, mirrors, pizza warmers, and much-improved washrooms. But in addition to the cosmetic facelift, The Wicked Wedge has improved the quality of the ingredients and now incorporates organic, hand-pitted olives and better cheese. At the same time, they have kept their trademark crust and their lively tomato sauce. Much of this may be lost on the clientele who frequent the joint at 3 am after the bars unload, but for those of us who drop by during less bleary hours, it's a positive move.

The improvements can be credited to new owners—sisters Kelci and Leah Norton and their aunt, Gail Norton. Gail has years of experience running The Cookbook Co., and she knows a good olive when she sees one.

So for a good and affordable slice at almost any time of day, The Wicked Wedge stands the test of time.

www.thewickedwedge.com

Address
618–17 Avenue SW

Phone
228·1024

Hours
Monday–Wednesday
11 am–midnight

Thursday–Saturday
11 am–close

Sunday
noon–10 pm

Reservations
Not accepted

Cards
V, MC, AE, Debit

Drinks
No alcoholic beverages

Takeout
Yes
Delivery

Outdoor Dining
Benches for 10

Wiener Schnitzel Haus

Austrian

SOMETIMES you just need a good schnitzel. So where are you going to get one? Perhaps at Wiener Schnitzel Haus, where they do pork or chicken schnitzel and serve them with Austrian salads and goulash soup.

Wiener Schnitzel Haus is a surprising little spot in the heart of Montgomery, the former village that many people traverse westerly on their way out of town. Wiener Schnitzel used to be a fast-food joint and still carries some vestiges of its past—the long ordering counter, the overhead menu, the orange-ish tones. But the owner is slowly upgrading the old look. The plastic booths have been removed in favour of tables, some plants have been added, and a wine list has been created.

The result is a simple and pleasant thirty-four-seat cafe with tastes of Austria. Most schnitzels—the basic one with cabbage slaw, for instance, the Jaeger schnitzel with wild mushroom sauce, and the filled schnitzel with brie and pear—are priced in the mid-teens and come as substantial meals with salads and spaetzle. The meat is breaded and fried and served hot and crisp. It's not at all greasy. You'd pay much more for this food in fancier restaurants—if we had fancier Austrian restaurants in Calgary, that is.

So with a little apple strudel for dessert, Wiener Schnitzel Haus can quell those schnitzel needs. At least for a while.

Address
4703 Bowness Road NW

Phone
288·2230

Hours
Tuesday–Friday
4 pm–8 pm

Saturday
noon–8 pm

Reservations
Accepted for groups
of 6 or more

Cards
V, MC, Debit

Drinks
Beer & wine only
Corkage $10

Takeout
Yes

Outdoor Dining
No

Wild Flour | Bakery Cafe

WILD Flour closes one day a week in winter just so the staff can go snowboarding. It's that kind of place. Organic everything—flour, coffee, fruits, vegetables, meats. But when the snow goes—sometime in May—it's back to work every day.

Because folks want their waffles ($6), their granola ($3.50), and their ham-gruyere-sage sandwiches on crusty bread ($7).Wild Flour is a natural for Banff, a spot for a coffee in a sunlit, ecologically built development or a casual soup-and-sandwich lunch or an afternoon tea with scones. To taste it all, Wild Flour serves an $11 lunch special of a half-sandwich, a bowl of soup, a cup of coffee, and a cookie. That'll keep you going.

The twenty-eight seats inside Wild Flour—and the patio in warmer weather—seem to be constantly full. Folks line up at the counter to select their meals to eat in and their baking to take home. Organic Kicking Horse and Cafe Femenino coffees are brewed at a separate station, and you can see the bakers toiling away through a large window.

Wild Flour is an integral piece of The Bison Courtyard complex, which includes The Bison Mountain Bistro. The Flour children also run Glacier Lily, an organic ice cream and juice operation in the Courtyard that was barely open at press time. Check with Wild Flour for more info.

www.wildflourbakery.ca

Address
211 Bear Street
(The Bison Courtyard)
Banff

Phone
760·5074

Hours
Mid-May–mid-October:
Daily
7 am–7 pm

Mid-October–mid-May:
Wednesday–Monday
7 am–7 pm

Reservations
Not accepted

Cards
V, MC, Debit

Drinks
No alcoholic beverages

Takeout
Yes

Outdoor Dining
Patio

Wild Horse Bistro

WHEN you put risotto, quesadillas, tandoori pork, and lamb with tzatziki sauce on the menu, how do you define the food style? Innovative would be one word. As in Innovative Alberta Cuisine, according to Amy and Jesse Smulders, the two cheerful sisters who own Black Diamond's Wild Horse Bistro. They studied under Mark Klaudt of the neighbouring Route 40 Soup Co., and they've now taken Alberta cuisine in their own unique direction.

Works for me. Especially when you include a blue-cheese-topped elk burger, smoked trout pâté, and hearty soups made from local produce and served with cornbread. (And then you keep most things under $12.) These gals are as creative as they are charming, and they see few boundaries to their cuisine. If it tastes good, they go for it. I've even ordered a big salad here just to see what they might throw in.

At press time, they had just introduced their first breakfast menu. It includes gluten-free waffles, low-fat and sugar-free baking, smoothies, and good old bacon and eggs.

The result of their efforts is a tiny cafe where everyone seems comfortable. And where, it seems, almost half of Black Diamond's population can be found socializing and enjoying a tasty meal at any given time. (The other half are waiting for the first half to finish so they can get a table.)

But no one's in a big hurry. There's dessert to consider. Maybe cheesecake or chocolate zucchini cake. After lunch settles a bit, that is. In the meantime, there's always more visiting to do.

www.wildhorsebistro.ca

Address
126 Centre Avenue
Black Diamond

Phone
933·5800

Hours
Monday–Thursday
7:30 am–3 pm

Friday
7:30 am–3 pm
5:30 pm–9 pm

Saturday
11 am–9 pm

Sunday
noon–8 pm

Reservations
Accepted for Friday &
Saturday only

Cards
V, MC, Debit

Drinks
Fully licensed
Corkage $10

Takeout
Yes

Outdoor Dining
2 tables

More Buffets

CAN'T get enough buffets? Me neither. There are a number in this book, but in the spirit of the multi-course smorgasbord, here are eleven more that deserve notice. You can order off the menu at these places too, but then you'd probably be over my cheap-eats budget. (That's why these restaurants don't each have their own page in this book.) Note: These are all lunch buffets.

### Delhi Darbar	Indian
Northern Indian and contemporary Delhi dishes in this little place across from the Glenmore Inn.	2742 Glenmore Trail SE 720·6669 Monday–Friday, $11.95

### Karma	Indian
A stylish space in South Trail Crossing with a good Northern Indian buffet that includes some Hakka dishes too.	309, 4600–130 Avenue SE 257·4977 Monday–Friday, $11.95

### Leo Fu's	Chinese
Szechuan and Mandarin selections at this fine Chinese restaurant just off Macleod Trail.	511–70 Avenue SW 255·2528 Monday–Thursday, $8.50 Friday, $8.95

### Rose Garden	Thai
The best deal for a Stephen Avenue buffet. Reserve well ahead. It's busy, busy.	112 Stephen Avenue SW (Second Floor) 264·1988 Monday–Friday, $13.95

### Ruan Thai	Thai
A high-quality Thai buffet in the Beltline, and a relaxing respite from the busy streets of the area.	101, 1324–11 Avenue SW 262·7066 Monday–Friday, $12.25

Sahara | Lebanese

A Lebanese buffet with some Western selections at this downtown, downstairs location.

739–2 Avenue SW
(Downstairs)
262•7222
Monday–Friday, $13.99

Surya | Indian

This Northern Indian buffet packs a punch. Careful with the address, though—the entrance is on 12th Street SW.

101, 1207–11 Avenue SW
290•1777
Monday–Friday, $12.99

Thai Boat | Thai

Wednesdays only for this Thai buffet in one of the few non-chain joints along 32nd Avenue NE.

108, 2323–32 Avenue NE
291•9887
Wednesday, $11.99

Thai Nongkhai | Thai

The buffet is only on Tuesdays at this cousin of Thai Boat, so plan ahead for Thai Nongkhai's smorg.

10, 7400 Macleod Trail S
705•3329
Tuesday, $13.95

Thai Place East | Thai

Located in the Best Western Airport Inn, Thai Place East does an excellent Thai buffet.

1947–18 Avenue NE
291•4148
Monday–Friday, $12.95

Thai Place West | Thai

In the Motel Village Quality Inn, Thai Place West fills the air—and your stomach—with fine Thai food.

2359 Banff Trail NW
338•4405
Monday–Friday, $12.95

More Coffee (and Tea too)

Do good coffee shops really belong in this book? (The question itself may be offensive to some.) Even though the most expensive cup of joe is still under $5, that's not really lunch or dinner, is it? Still, I'd like to include a few more of my favourite beverage stops. Like many of the individual coffee shops that get a whole page to themselves in this book, most of these offer good and reasonably priced food. I just didn't have enough pages to go around. And I was already buzzed on caffeine.

Beamers

Good coffee and mega-muffins at two locations in Canmore. They brew custom coffee blends here, like their Old Goat and their Junkyard. Tasty!

737–7 Avenue
Canmore
609·0111

1702 Bow Valley Trail
Canmore
678·3988

Caffe Beano

A Calgary classic, Beano expanded in 2007 and is as busy as ever. (Try the molasses muffins.)

1613–9 Street SW
229·1232

Caffe Rosso

A new coffee shop in Ramsay Exchange, the former Dominion Bridge building, with crisp panini too.

803–24 Avenue SE
479·2999

Heartland

Two locations—one rustic-historic, one contemporary-ecological—both with good coffee and a pleasant community feel.

940–2 Avenue NW
270·4541

116–7A Street NE
263·4567

Oolong Tea House

Black teas, white teas, green teas, oolong teas. Even Earl Grey rooibus, the newest tea trend, is available here.

110–10 Street NW
283·0333

Phil & Sebastian

Behind the high-tech machines and fancy espresso beans lie a commitment to the best coffee possible. (Only open Friday through Sunday, though.)

4421 Quesnay Wood Drive SW
(Calgary Farmers' Market)
612·2266

Purple Perk

This always-busy Mission-area coffee shop brews fine coffee and makes some tasty squares too.

2212–4 Street SW
244·1300

The Roasterie

You can smell the coffee roasting from blocks away, and when you arrive, it tastes as sweet and rich and dark as you had hoped.

314–10 Street NW
270·3304

Steeps

Urban and urbane, Steeps serves superb tea in the pot or by the leaf. Their masala chai is a huge seller.

880–16 Avenue SW
(Mount Royal Village)
209·0076

Tutti Frutti

Henry and Debbie Mandelbaum brew fine coffee to go along with Calgary's best gelato, addictive house-baked cookies, and their always smiling faces. (Also only open Friday through Sunday.)

4421 Quesnay Wood Drive SW
(Calgary Farmers' Market)
889·5969

More Markets

THERE's nothing like shopping for food to make a person hungry. Whether it's a farmers' market, for instance, or a bagel shop or a Middle Eastern store, I often feel the need for a nosh while hunting and gathering. There are other markets in this book with full-page entries, but I didn't want to leave these favourites out.

Avenue Deli

Slice off a pound or two of smoked meat, or sit and enjoy a sandwich and shake at this small Marda Loop shop.

3, 2008–33 Avenue SW
242·6783

Billingsgate

A bowl of chowder or a quick fish and chips at Billingsgate Seafood Market while trawling for mussels and salmon always satisfies.

2B, 1941 Uxbridge Drive NW
269·3474

The Daily Bagel

Great smoked meat sandwiches—with pickles 'n' chips—at this market kiosk. There are also bagels to buy from Montreal Bagels and pounds of coffee from Kicking Horse.

4421 Quesnay Wood Drive SW
(Calgary Farmers' Market)
990·3431

Franca's

At the back of this Italian gift shop (where the gifts are mostly high-end Italian foods), there is a fine panini bar with great desserts and espresso too.

2404B Edmonton Trail NE
277·0766

Lina's Italian Market

Lina's is a fine place to pick up provolone and prosciutto and peppers or enjoy them all on a pizza in her cafe after shopping.

2202 Centre Street N
277·9166

The Main Dish

Mostly an upscale, urban-focused, take-home market, The Main Dish also offers fresh soups, sandwiches, and salads to eat in.

903 General Avenue NE
265·3474

Margarita's Dishes

Want a blintz? Or a bowl of borscht direct from the Ukraine? Check out Margarita's for food like baba made. (If your baba was from the Ukraine, that is.)

4421 Quesnay Wood Drive SW
(Calgary Farmers' Market)
244·4548

Mediterranea

Jimmy Elrafih's Middle Eastern market in the Beltline serves a good shawarma while you're picking up olives and tabbouleh to-go.

1304–4 Street SW
264·3424

Montreal Bagels

Montreal Bagels makes only two kinds of sandwiches—smoked meat and smoked salmon—but it can still be a tough choice. Maybe one of each to go along with a bag of fresh St.-Viateur-style bagels.

8408 Elbow Drive SW
212·4060

Somar

This Middle Eastern market slices up shawarma and donair to go along with their dry goods and Montreal-baked desserts.

17, 9250 Macleod Trail S
252·2700

Wayne's Bagels

Wayne moved to Macleod Trail recently, but he stills bakes his bagels in a wood-fired oven and makes some good sandwiches too.

104, 4515 Macleod Trail S
270·7090

The Lists

THESE lists will guide you to various geographic areas and food styles. Most eateries are arranged alphabetically in the book. When they are not, the lists will direct you with one of two kinds of *see* references: Either you will be directed to another eatery that is, in fact, in alphabetical order or you will be directed to More Buffets on pages 110 to 111; More Coffee (and Tea too) on pages 112 to 113; or More Markets on pages 114 to 115.

All establishments are in Calgary unless noted otherwise.

Northeast Calgary

Aamu
Boccavino
Bon Appetit
Boogie's Burgers
Clay Oven
Diner Deluxe
Fat Kee
Franca's (*see* More Markets)
Heartland (*see* More Coffee)
Joycee's
King's
Lina's Italian Market (*see* More Markets)
Little Italy
Main Dish, The (*see* More Markets)
Pimento's
Roti Hut, The
Shikiji
Sushi Hibiki
Taketomi Village
Tazza
Thai Boat (*see* More Buffets)
Thai Place East (*see* More Buffets)
Uyen Uyen
Wonton King (*see* King's)

Northwest Calgary

A & A Deli
Billingsgate (*see* More Markets)
Boca Loca
Cadence
Central Blends
Dairy Lane
Dell Cafe
Gunkan
Hawkwood Palace
Heartland (*see* More Coffee)
Higher Ground
Istanbul
Kaffee Stube
Lazy Loaf & Kettle
Niko's Bistro
Oolong Tea House (*see* More Coffee)
Pelican Pier
Peppino
Roasterie, The (*see* More Coffee)
Shawarma Station
Thai Place West (*see* More Markets)
Wiener Schnitzel Haus

Southeast Calgary

Baba Ka Dhaba
Babylon
Blackfoot Diner
Caffe Rosso (*see* More Coffee)
China Rose
Cravings
Delhi Darbar (*see* More Buffets)
DinoRosa's

eat! eat! in Inglewood
Ironwood
Karma (*see* More Buffets)
Miss Avril's
Pho Binh Minh
Pies Plus
Rincón Latino
Rocky's Burgers
Somar (*see* More Markets)
Spolumbo's
Thai Nongkhai (*see* More
  Buffets)
Tiffin
Ukrainian Fine Foods
Village Pita
Wonton King (*see* King's)

Southwest Calgary

Avenue Deli (*see* More
  Markets)
Belmont Diner (*see* Galaxie
  Diner)
Caffe Beano (*see* More Coffee)
Crete Souvlaki
Daily Bagel, The (*see* More
  Markets)
Il Centro
Kinjo
Leo Fu's (*see* More Buffets)
Little Chef
Margarita's Dishes (*see* More
  Markets)
Mediterranean Grill
Mi Tierra
Montreal Bagels (*see* More
  Markets)
Pfanntastic Pannenkoek
Phil & Sebastian (*see* More
  Coffee)
Primal Grounds
Tommy Burger Bar
Tutti Frutti (*see* More Coffee)
Wayne's Bagels (*see* More
  Markets)

Beltline/Mission

Aida's
Avellino's Panini
Boca Loca
Bumpy's
Caffe Beano (*see* More Coffee)
Color Tinto
Falafel King
Fat Tony's
Flatlands
Galaxie Diner
Holy Grill, The
Kawa Espresso Bar (*see* Java
  Jamboree)
Koi
Le Chien Chaud
Lion's Den
Mediterranea (*see* More
  Markets)
Mirchi
Mt. Everest's Kitchen
Oishii Village
Palace of Eats
Purple Perk (*see* More Coffee)
Ruan Thai (*see* More Buffets)
Rustic Sourdough
Saigon
Steeps (*see* More Coffee)
Surya (*see* More Buffets)
Tubby Dog
Vogglio D'Pizza
Wicked Wedge, The

Downtown Calgary

*atomic
Atlas
Avellino's Panini
Avenue Diner
Falafel King
Jonas' Restaurant
Luxor
Pimento's
Prairie Ink
Rose Garden (*see* More
  Buffets)
Sahara (*see* More Buffets)

Silver Dragon
Smokee Lee's
Trung Nguyen

Banff/Lake Louise

Barpa Bill's (Banff)
Bison General Store, The
    (Banff)
Laggan's (Lake Louise)
Pad Thai (Banff)
Silver Dragon (Banff)
Wild Flour (Banff)

Canmore

Beamers (*see* More Coffee)
Communitea
Gourmet Croissant
Harvest
JK Bakery
Miné
Railway Deli
Thai Pagoda (*see* Pad Thai)
Valbella Cafe

Foothills/Beyond

Chuckwagon (Turner Valley)
High Country Cafe
    (Millarville)
Java Jamboree (Cochrane)
Marv's (Black Diamond)
Route 40 Soup Co. (Turner
    Valley)
South Fork (High River)
Wild Horse Bistro (Black
    Diamond)

Austrian/German/Swiss

JK Bakery (Canmore)
Kaffee Stube
Railway Deli (Canmore)
Rustic Sourdough
Valbella Cafe (Canmore)
Wiener Schnitzel Haus

Bakeries

Gourmet Croissant
    (Canmore)
JK Bakery (Canmore)
Lazy Loaf & Kettle
Montreal Bagels (*see* More
    Markets)
Pies Plus
Rustic Sourdough
Village Pita
Wayne's Bagels (*see* More
    Markets)
Wild Flour (Banff)

Breakfast/Brunch
(*see also* Diners, p. 120)

Bon Appetit
Bumpy's
Cadence
Central Blends
Chuckwagon (Turner Valley)
Color Tinto
Communitea (Canmore)
Cravings
Dairy Lane
eat! eat! in Inglewood
Flatlands
Harvest (Canmore)
High Country Cafe
    (Millarville)
Higher Ground
Java Jamboree (Cochrane)
Laggan's (Lake Louise)
Little Chef
Pfanntastic Pannenkoek
Pies Plus
Primal Grounds
Railway Deli (Canmore)
Silver Dragon (Banff &
    Calgary)
South Fork (High River)
Wild Flour (Banff)
Wild Horse Bistro (Black
    Diamond)

Buffets

(see also More Buffets, pp. 110–111)

Aamu
China Rose
Clay Oven
Mt. Everest's Kitchen

Burgers/Dogs

Boogie's Burgers
Holy Grill, The
Le Chien Chaud
Marv's (Black Diamond)
Rocky's Burgers
Tommy Burger Bar
Tubby Dog

Canadian

Avenue Diner
Belmont Diner (*see* Galaxie Diner)
Bison General Store, The (Banff)
Bon Appetit
Boogie's Burgers
Cadence
Chuckwagon (Turner Valley)
Daily Bagel, The (*see* More Markets)
Dairy Lane
eat! eat! in Inglewood
Flatlands
Galaxie Diner
Harvest (Canmore)
High Country Cafe (Millarville)
King's
Lazy Loaf & Kettle
Little Chef
Palace of Eats
Pelican Pier
Prairie Ink
Route 40 Soup Co. (Turner Valley)
Smokee Lee's

South Fork (High River)
Tommy Burger Bar
Wild Horse Bistro (Black Diamond)

Caribbean

Joycee's
Miss Avril's
Roti Hut, The

Chinese

China Rose
Dell Cafe
Fat Kee
Hawkwood Palace
King's
Leo Fu's (*see* More Buffets)
Silver Dragon (Banff & Calgary)
Taketomi Village
Wonton King (*see* King's)

Coffee/Tea

(see also More Coffee, pp. 112–113)

*atomic
Avellino's Panini
Bumpy's
Cadence
Central Blends
Communitea (Canmore)
Higher Ground
Java Jamboree (Cochrane)
Kawa Espresso Bar (*see* Java Jamboree)
Primal Grounds

Contemporary

*atomic
Avenue Diner
Bison General Store, The (Banff)
Diner Deluxe
Flatlands

Ironwood
Koi
Main Dish, The (*see* More Markets)
Route 40 Soup Co. (Turner Valley)
Wild Flour (Banff)
Wild Horse Bistro (Black Diamond)

Delis

A & A Deli
Avenue Deli (*see* More Markets)
Babylon
Little Italy
Luxor
Peppino
Pimento's
Rustic Sourdough
Valbella Cafe (Canmore)

Diners

Avenue Diner
Belmont Diner (*see* Galaxie Diner)
Blackfoot Diner
Dell Cafe
Diner Deluxe
Galaxie Diner
Lion's Den
Marv's (Black Diamond)
Palace of Eats

Fishy

Billingsgate (*see* More Markets)
Gunkan
Kinjo
Oishii Village
Pelican Pier
Shikiji
Sushi Hibiki

Greek

Barpa Bill's (Banff)
Crete Souvlaki

Indian/Pakistani

Baba Ka Dhaba
Clay Oven
Delhi Darbar (*see* More Buffets)
Karma (*see* More Buffets)
Mirchi
Surya (*see* More Buffets)
Taketomi Village
Tiffin

Italian/Pizza

Avellino's Panini
Boccavino
DinoRosa's
Fat Tony's
Franca's (*see* More Markets)
Il Centro
Lina's Italian Market (*see* More Markets)
Little Italy
Niko's Bistro
Peppino
Pimento's
Spolumbo's
Vogglio D'Pizza
Wicked Wedge, The

Japanese

Gunkan
Kinjo
Miné (Canmore)
Oishii Village
Shikiji
Sushi Hibiki

Latin American

Boca Loca
Color Tinto

Mi Tierra
Rincón Latino
Vogglio D'Pizza

Somar (*see* More Markets)
Tazza
Village Pita

Markets

(*see also* More Markets,
pp. 114–115)

Boca Loca
DinoRosa's
Joycee's
Kaffee Stube
Mi Tierra
Peppino's
Railway Deli (Canmore)

Meaty

Atlas
Boogie's Burgers
Holy Grill, The
Kaffee Stube
Le Chien Chaud
Marv's (Black Diamond)
Palace of Eats
Railway Deli (Canmore)
Rocky's Burgers
Shawarma Station
Smokee Lee's
Spolumbo's
Tommy Burger Bar
Tubby Dog
Valbella Cafe (Canmore)
Wiener Schnitzel Haus

Middle Eastern

A & A Deli
Aida's
Babylon
Falafel King
Istanbul
Luxor
Mediterranea (*see* More
    Markets)
Mediterranean Grill
Sahara (*see* More Buffets)
Shawarma Station

One of a Kind

Aamu (Afghani)
Atlas (Persian)
Ironwood (Upscale Pub Food/
    Roadhouse)
Jonas' Restaurant
    (Hungarian)
Mt. Everest's Kitchen
    (Nepalese)
Pfanntastic Pannenkoek
    (Dutch Pancakes)
Ukrainian Fine Foods
    (Ukrainian)

Thai

Pad Thai (Banff)
Rose Garden (*see* More
    Buffets)
Ruan Thai (*see* More Buffets)
Thai Boat (*see* More Buffets)
Thai Nongkhai (*see* More
    Buffets)
Thai Pagoda (Canmore, *see*
    Pad Thai)
Thai Place East (*see* More
    Buffets)
Thai Place West (*see* More
    Buffets)

Vegetarian

Aida's
Clay Oven
Cravings
Falafel King
Hawkwood Palace
Koi
Luxor
Mediterranean Grill
Mirchi
Mt. Everest's Kitchen
Prairie Ink

Tazza
Tiffin
Wild Flour (Banff)
Wild Horse Bistro (Black
  Diamond)

Vietnamese

Pho Binh Minh
Saigon
Trung Nguyen
Uyen Uyen

My Cheapest 10

Baba Ka Dhaba
Blackfoot Diner
Bon Appetit
Crete Souvlaki
Fat Kee
Pho Binh Minh
Rustic Sourdough
Taketomi Village
Trung Nguyen
Ukrainian Fine Foods

My Favourite 22

Aida's
Atlas
Avenue Diner
Barpa Bill's (Banff)
Bumpy's
Clay Oven
Diner Deluxe
Galaxie Diner
Gourmet Croissant (Canmore)
Il Centro
Istanbul
Jonas' Restaurant
Kinjo
Lion's Den
Little Chef
Mt. Everest's Kitchen
Pfanntastic Pannenkoek
Pies Plus
Rocky's Burgers
Route 40 Soup Co. (Turner
  Valley)
Saigon
Spolumbo's